ORIGINAL SETTINGS

BECOME AN INNER ENGINEER OF YOUR MIND AND HEART

JORGE L. CABAN

WESTBOW
PRESS®
A DIVISION OF THOMAS NELSON
& ZONDERVAN

This book is a work of non-fiction. Unless otherwise noted, the author and the publisher make no explicit guarantees as to the accuracy of the information contained in this book and in some cases, names of people and places have been altered to protect their privacy.

WestBow Press books may be ordered through booksellers or by contacting:

WestBow Press
A Division of Thomas Nelson & Zondervan
1663 Liberty Drive
Bloomington, IN 47403
www.westbowpress.com
844-714-3454

Because of the dynamic nature of the Internet, any web addresses or links contained in this book may have changed since publication and may no longer be valid. The views expressed in this work are solely those of the author and do not necessarily reflect the views of the publisher, and the publisher hereby disclaims any responsibility for them.

Any people depicted in stock imagery provided by Getty Images are models, and such images are being used for illustrative purposes only.
Certain stock imagery © Getty Images.

ISBN: 979-8-3850-0796-7 (sc)
ISBN: 979-8-3850-0797-4 (hc)
ISBN: 979-8-3850-0798-1 (e)

Library of Congress Control Number: 2023917641

Print information available on the last page.

WestBow Press rev. date: 12/04/2023

CONTENTS

Introduction ix

Chapter 1   The creator created creation to create 1
Chapter 2   Cultivating the Garden of Our Hearts 15
Chapter 3   The Inner Worlds 23
Chapter 4   The Inception of Self 41
Chapter 5   Witches Warlocks & Occult 48
Chapter 6   Proof is in the Pudding 58
Chapter 7   Inner Conversation Create Reality 68
Chapter 8   The Lookout 74
Chapter 9   Passcodes and Programs 86
Chapter 10   The Art of Harpu 97
Chapter 11   Harpu Day and Night Practice 110
Chapter 12   Programming Your Heart 137

INTRODUCTION

My name is Jorge L. Caban, and I feel compelled to share the incredible journey that led to the creation of this book. It all began in 2016 when, during a period of deep prayer and fasting, I received a divine directive from the Lord. He instructed me to embark on a 21-day fast, completely alone, and to start writing. And so, with unwavering faith, I began this extraordinary endeavor.

The very first words that flowed from my pen were the title of the book: Original Settings. Little did I know then, that these writing sessions would become a regular part of my life. At the start of each year, I was led to set myself apart and continue this sacred practice. Over the course of the next seven years, I undertook five 21-day fasts in water, one 30-day fast in water only, and even a 40-day fast in Costa Rica, also in water only.

It is through this deep search for truth, during those moments of devoted introspection and connection with the divine, that the revelations for this book took shape. The profound insights and wisdom gained during these periods of fasting and writing have become the foundation of Original Settings.

My personal story that is the fuel for this book began in Newark, New Jersey, where my life experiences would take a significant shift in my surroundings at a very young age. Moving from a close-knit community to a different area brought about many cultural and economic changes. It was a difficult transition, especially during my formative years when I craved independence and freedom.

During this time, I faced numerous hardships that would change the trajectory of my life. From being picked on to enduring bullying and even physical assaults, the world seemed like a constant battleground. It took a toll on my character and transformed me into a survivalist, always on guard, always expecting an attack from every corner. Unfortunately, I will live my life this way for many years to come.

I just recently found out emotional trauma is not what made me that way but rather, the inability to process such emotions. Understanding that now, I can see the little boy version of myself doing the best he could with the tools he had. I became this rigid, hard-hearted, emotionless person who would become a man harboring all of these negative attributes that he didn't know how to change.

My new environment in Central Newark altered my direction in life quickly and drove me down an alley that would ultimately lead me to drugs at sixteen, in an attempt to escape my emotional trauma. I developed coping mechanisms that would destroy the following ten years of my life. I started smoking marijuana and then started selling to continue my habit. I ventured deeper into the drug world and rapidly advanced to using heroin. I found myself in random, abandoned buildings. I lost everything, including my family and loved ones. Unfortunately, it took me almost overdosing in a hotel room for me to decide that I needed to change my life and seek help. I realized that this was not God's original plan for me.

I went through the 12-step program of Narcotics Anonymous and I spent two years in upstate New York in a program called the Salvation Army. After completing both of these milestones, I finally had enough strength to come back and face my demons in my hometown of Central Newark. Coming back, I was able to begin spreading light to the dark areas of my life and restoring all that I had lost, but I still felt like something was missing, specifically in my spiritual life. I knew of God but I didn't truly know God.

In my spiritual journey, I dove into witchcraft at 26 and continued practicing it for 10 years. I was content performing rituals and felt satisfied with my spirituality until I began to see dark sides of me creeping up from the past, specifically my addiction. I remember traveling to the Dominican Republic, For what would be the last time to visit the medium, I told her "There was an empty place in my heart which of the saints can fill that void?" Her response was, "I don't have someone for that," which marked a turning point for me that led me to begin looking for someone who could fill me.

When I returned from the Dominican Republic, I pleaded with God and said "If you're real, come and get me." Out of desperation, I was a lost sheep calling out for its shepherd. At that moment, it felt like my mouth was released to shout out the cry of my heart. For the next seven days in my home, my bed would sporadically shake, doors were opening and closing on their own, the sink faucet would come on without being turned on, and the TV would start on its own at 3:00 a.m. It felt like an exorcist movie. My 12-year-old son at the time can attest to these spiritual encounters. I had not slept for almost seven days. I was taking ten Advil PM pills and still had problems sleeping, and I was also dealing with sleep paralysis. After that week, I remember getting ready to take a walk to try and clear my mind. When I stepped out of my home, walking across the street. I was immediately met by a woman in a red 1999 Ford Explorer Coup. She rolled down her car window and said, "You called, here I am." When I heard her say those words, my body shivered as if my spirit recognized the voice. She went on to tell me about the office where I worked and the saints that I worshiped, mentioning each one by name. She told me of the food that gave me heartburn and even described the two women in my life, saying that one had dark skin, while the other had light skin. She said the woman with dark skin is the one you have a child with, while currently, you're with another woman with red hair. You can imagine my reaction. After that, I exchanged a few more words with this mysterious prophet. She told me that she would return at 7:30 p.m. to pick me up and go to church with her. For some reason, I will never fully understand why I agreed to go with her but I did because internally I was compelled to do so. And this crazy story is how my journey with God began. And what a journey it has been getting back to my original settings.

My transformation occurred as I experienced a close walk with God in intimacy, where I realized that there are layers to trauma and I had to dig through these layers to experience God's freedom truly. One of the ways I began to excavate my dark past was by praying and fasting and eventually hearing the voice of God and following instructions. One of the instructions was that I would be invited to the Dominican Republic and I was to take the invitation. While I was there, God gave me specific instructions to go up a mountain and pray at midnight. The mountain we ascended was called the mountain of deliverance. On that hiking journey, the Bible became real to me. No longer was the story of a man squealing like a pig being delivered from evil spirits just a passage to me. I became that man squealing like a pig as I was being delivered supernaturally from dark forces within me. But even within the state of being shifted from the kingdom of darkness to the kingdom of light, I felt in my heart there was more. I believe God puts a hunger, a desire for him in us so that we can continue seeking him. In the biblical book of Jeremiah, it says seek him, and you shall find him when you seek him with all your heart.

The journey doesn't stop there, another life-changing encounter that helped me witness more of God's freedom and give birth to this book occurred when I went away to Wellsprings Ministries. I have a friend of mine who I call Prophet Chris Allen, whom God used to navigate me in the right direction. He contacted me one day and asked to have lunch together. While we sat and ate, he turned to me and said there's somewhere I want you to go to. My internal conversation was coated in curiosity as I wondered what he was going to ask me. He said, "I went to this healing school in Alaska that has to do with a deeper level of freedom. I was transformed there. God has called you for deliverance, to help set people free emotionally, so I believe God wants to take you there. And I want you to go." I looked at him and said, "You're crazy." and officially changed his name to Crazy Chris. I insisted that I was not going to Alaska and began listing reasons why I couldn't. "I'm not in a position to go to Alaska. I can't afford it. I don't have anybody there, it's cold and I'm not going. Please don't ask me again." Fortunately, we continued to meet up and talk about this potential Alaska trip. During our fourth lunch, Chris pulled out his computer and asked for my contact info, including my address. Little did I know, he was booking my reservation for Alaska and this trip that would catapult my life, ministry, and well-being.

When I first got there, I continued to complain. I was struggling to adjust to the weather and kept arguing with Chris about making me go to Alaska, but deep inside I knew that it was where God wanted me to be at the time. After the first day's orientation, I tried to be more present and leave behind my ego, stubbornness, and complaints. During the classes, I sat and listened, and since I had plenty of solitary time, I could apply what I was learning. Could it be that this was the missing link I needed to complete what God wanted to do through my life?

By day three, I started to hear teachings about how the Holy Spirit is a counselor and how the Holy Spirit can show you the truth that you're unaware of. It was the first time in my life that I was taught the Holy Spirit worked in that manner internally, not just externally. So, like a little kid learning a new thing I went to my room and started asking the Holy Spirit to internally address the issues I had faced my whole life. I called them glitches in my avatar. Those glitches are buttons that we all feel like we have no control over. I started with anger. Now, I was considerably passive as a person, but some areas in my life were still dark. I always say a lot of people have 80% of their hearts in the light, but there is often 20% that still has some darkness, usually characterized by lies that we believe are true. It was midnight on my fourth day in Alaska and I asked the Holy Spirit the following question, "Holy Spirit, show me your truth concerning anger?" The experience I had in my room was uncanny.

For three hours, I was on my knees, and the Holy Spirit took me back to when I was ten years old, the first time I encountered trauma. I could even see the graffiti on the walls in my neighborhood in Newark. It was so detailed as if someone had taken a video recording of my life and decided to rewind and replay it 30 years later. Specific people came to my mind. I remembered their names and faces and what they did to me. I could feel the Holy Spirit telling me that I needed to forgive and release them. I needed to let them go because the only person in bondage was myself.

I continued attending the classes and often felt like a sponge. I tried to absorb as much as I could and came back dripping with wisdom. I was certified at the institution as an inner healer and I felt pretty confident that I had changed irreversibly, but the biggest test happened when I came back from Alaska a week later. I own properties in Newark and I had to address someone who needed to pay me rent that was backed up. I saw the person and usually, the unhealed and old Jorge was ready to attack him because I was still operating on the frozen trauma of the past ten-year-old Jorge. I would have angrily addressed this issue with force, however, I asked the person who owed me money if we could speak in the hallway. If you're familiar with urban areas, normally when someone calls you into a hallway, you do not enter, but he did. There was no hint of anger in my words, but only compassion and empathy towards him. He went on to tell me that at one point, he was a minister of God, but he lost his way. His life veered off into drugs and addiction. After he shared this with me, I merely asked him if he wanted any help with his issues, and he immediately responded with, "Yes, whatever it takes." I got him a ticket to Florida to attend a rehab center. He finished the rehab center after one year and as of today, is still free of drugs and delivered from darkness into light. I would have never responded with compassion and understanding if I had not gone to Alaska and dealt with my 20% of darkness.

Everything I've learned from that trip until now has helped me write this book. After my time in Alaska, I immediately came back to my church and shared with our team that we were going to start something called Matrix University, a teaching program made to help others experience inner healing and become whole. I've seen hundreds of people set free, reconcile with their past, and redeemed from their hurt because of the lessons I've shared with them after experiencing freedom firsthand. I've learned that they can still work to overcome those areas that are tormenting them, even though they already know God. I hope that as you read this book you take a clear observation of yourself and start changing not only your external situation but also your internal position.

Something I have learned is that mental health can take many forms. There's depression, anxiety, schizophrenia, addiction, and so on. Some challenges are more visible than others, and you might recognize them immediately. Others can be harder to see when you're not looking for them, but they are still there.

The healthcare industry only wants to care for you, not cure you, because you are a machine that produces money for them. It's an industry; therefore, they will continue giving you pills to care for you and make you feel better without taking care of the underlying issue. The result is that they rarely cure you.

These statistics provide a look at how many people face mental health whether we see it or not

- In the United States, almost half of all adults (46.4 percent) will experience a mental illness during their lifetime.
- Approximately 5 percent of adults (eighteen or older) experience a mental illness in any one year; this is equivalent to 43.8 million people.

- Of adults in the United States with any mental disorder in one year, 14.4 percent have one condition, 5.8 percent have two disorders, and 6 percent have three or more.
- Half of all mental disorders begin by age fourteen, and three-quarters by age twenty-four.
- In the United States, only 41 percent of people with a mental disorder in the past year received professional health care.

Most of these disorders come from unprocessed emotional trauma. When we're born, we have everything in us to accomplish what God has intended for us. However, while growing up, many digress from their original settings, mostly not for their fault. This phrase, "Original Settings," is one I have come to use to characterize the original way in which God created humanity. We are wired for love, anything outside of this is an altered setting. Just like a tech company designs a phone with the latest specs and programs to operate at peak performance, God designed us with everything we need to reach and operate at our maximum potential on earth through love. This book was written to help us get back to the original settings that we were created with. But it must be stressed that as long as we live within our original settings, we are programmed for maximum results - nothing else is needed.

God has equipped us with everything we need to be successful. However, those settings are often changed not by choice but because of culture, fears, dogma, and other circumstances that contribute to a change in our original settings. This change occurs not always for success but for failure. The question is, what can we do about this?

You may ask yourself, "Is this what God has for me? Is this his best, or is there something I can do to regain my original settings?" - Yes, there is hope, and I pray that this book will be a blessing and a guide for you to return to your original settings. That being said, let's begin!

CHAPTER 1

THE CREATOR CREATED CREATION TO CREATE

"In the beginning, God created the heavens and earth," Genesis 1:1 (NIV).

I don't know if you believe in the Bible, as I do, but I have found some answers there, which will be a good starting point for us. All of creation comes to a point of searching for the creator. Science and spirituality have not supported each other as strongly as it has in the last ten years, unlike at any other time in history.

Science keeps pointing to God as the Creator of all creation. Some call God "energy," "the universe," "the light," or just "God." This brings me to the following questions: Was the beginning in his mind? Did he see it before he spoke it? or is it two rocks that collided and created perfection? This can be open for debates but let's be open-minded to where all the fingers are pointed to.

Let's see what the Bible says and what science keeps pointing to. Where they align, they both tell us that our most powerful tool is to be God-like in imagination. Please stop for a second and grasp how powerful that is. Nothing happens just on its own. We must first be intentional about designing in our imagination. - That is where it all begins.

"Faith shows the reality of what we hope for; it is the evidence of things we cannot see. Through their faith, the people in the days of old earned a good reputation. By faith, we understand that the entire universe was formed at God's command, that what we now see did not come from anything that can be seen." (Hebrews 11:1-3 NLT)

We read here that faith is believing in the substance of things hoped for and refers to what you desire. It is what you design in your mind but cannot see (yet) physically. It is still in the landscape of your mind from where everything is created. God designed in his mind what he wanted to see in the physical world, He created us like him.

Picture your mind as a canvas painted with your thoughts. We can be the artists of what appears on our canvases, but we often hand the paintbrush to others. When we give others the paintbrush, they design our future landscape. What this implies is that we don't always control our destiny. Whoever we allow to hold the paintbrush of our minds has that power! We must constantly ask ourselves, "Who holds my paintbrush? Am I painting my future, or is someone else painting negativity on my canvas?" And what is this canvas? - It is our mind, and we paint with the power of our imagination.

Our creativity starts before we physically see it. The Bible continues to say that God spoke and designed the visible with his words "By faith, we understand that the universe was created by the word of God so that what is seen was not made from things that are visible" (Hebrews 11:3 ESV).

God created what he had in his imagination and put it into words. He spoke out his design. Therefore, the most powerful thing God created is the mind. It is the ability to create with our imagination, just like him. In our consciousness, the mind is where we have the ability to create, and it is our greatest asset. Ideas start as invisible thoughts which become visible and manifest over time.

In Genesis 11:5-6 (KJV), the people gathered to create a tower to reach heaven. The Lord was so amazed by this creation that he had to come down to see what his creation had done. This story speaks about creation by applying principles established by God in the beginning by faith. In verse 6, the Lord said "Behold, the people are one, and they have all one language; and this they begin to do and now nothing will be restrained from them, which they have imagined doing." He realized that the people figured out how to use the unique imagination he deposited in all of them from the start of creation.

The keyword in this passage is imagined. God saw people's ability to create in their minds and bring forth whatever they fill their minds with. In other words, the blueprint of what they wanted to create was in their imagination. He decided nothing would be restrained from them, meaning what they see in their imagination would be seen in the physical, which many call to "manifest" something.

Science has reaffirmed this through recent studies. They had a subject think about something while viewing the inside of the subject's brain with Electron Microscopy (EM). They concluded that invisible thoughts become visible in the brain as the thoughts are being created. The ideas took up "mental real estate" in the subject's brain. This is called a synaptic connection. In other words, through neuro-pathways, we create a new reality. One can easily see why the ancient king of Israel, Solomon, said, "As a man thinks, so is He" (Proverbs 23:7 KJV).

In Sigmund Freud's psychoanalytic theory of personality, the conscious mind consists of everything inside our awareness. This aspect of our mental processing allows us to think and talk rationally. It's where our philosophy and our way of thinking originate. It's fueled by life experiences, past, present, and future. Likewise, it is also what we hear and what we see.

The conscious mind includes things such as

- Sensations
- Perceptions
- Memories
- Feelings
- Fantasies

Closely allied with the conscious mind is the subconscious mind. Our "second" mind is our original mind or as I describe it, the heart. It includes the things we are not thinking of currently but can quickly draw into conscious awareness. Think of a dangerous situation and how quickly you can respond without consciously thinking.

Things in the subconscious are available to the conscious mind only in a disguised form. Thoughts the conscious mind wants to keep hidden from awareness are repressed into the subconscious mind. While we are unaware of these feelings, thoughts, urges, and emotions all this happens in the invisible realm.

The long-term memory of the subconscious spills into awareness (conscious mind) in the form of actions, speech, and dreams from our past experiences, pain, hurt, or traumas. Past experiences influence almost all the decisions we make today. Our efforts and who we are in the conscious (mind) make up only 5 percent of our choices. The remaining 95 percent of our choices are driven by past programs, events, and moments tightly stored in the subconscious mind.

In reality, most of our life's choices are not caused by our current situation but by our past. The best way to explain this is to consider your subconscious mind as a library. Every book in the library is a significant moment in our lives that has a powerful emotional impact and is there, on the shelf, waiting for the right moment to spring into action. The decisions we make most of the time come from things already programmed inside our subconscious minds, spilling into our conscious minds.

Neuroscience teaches that the conscious mind processes about 50 bits of information per second, which is slower than our subconscious mind, which processes approximately 11,000,000 bits per second. This demonstrates how fast you can process information and recall the past. For example, when you make a statement such as, "Where did that come from?" after saying something negative or having a sudden insight. These thoughts occur from your subconscious and are brought forth into your awareness, the conscious mind.

The Power of Thoughts

Recently, I spoke with my cousin, who's into computers. He was telling me about virtual reality and how this technology will revolutionize the industry as we know it. A virtual reality experience of, let's say, riding a roller coaster invades your brain, which cannot distinguish whether the roller coaster ride is real or in the imagination. Your brain then releases the same chemicals to signal the body as if you're experiencing a roller-coaster ride in real time! It also can place someone for a moment in a distant place and have him or her experience that moment right where they are with the same emotional feeling as if he or she were indeed in a different location. That's how the conscious mind works. If we think about it, it becomes our virtual reality, even though it happened years ago or hasn't happened yet! We believe it to be, and then—bam!—it is.

Living in the past creates depression. Living in the future creates anxiety. But living in the now creates the peace we desire.

We are the creators of our present moment, Whether we create Calm or Chaos, thought alone creates it. What do we want this present moment to be? Are we going to create past regrets, anger, and bitterness or create calm and peace? We cannot allow our brain to continuously run on autopilot and release the wrong kind of chemicals that can destroy the body and keep us in a perpetuated stress mode ultimately leading to mental health issues and disease. We must take control. This is the aim of this book.

Did you know medical science has concluded that up to 80 percent of disease starts in our negative thought pattern? We create an environment for sickness by feeling negative emotions and sending our bodies into chaos. This chaos then leads to diseases. Unfortunately, while improving, today's medical training still aims to treat symptoms, not causes.

Have you ever been offended? Many times people encounter both large and small hurts from others whether they are aware of it or not. When we are offended, it creates discomfort, and we often retreat to a place in our past where we feel safe. To be in a state of discomfort is to be out of peace, and when we are out of peace, we open a door to sickness. We are often addicted to our past emotions, leading us back to a place of familiarity where we create familiar situations. These familiar emotions create an addiction to comfort that doesn't let us go without a fight.

We create a virtual reality whenever we experience a past trauma or presume the worst-case scenario. It happens in the mind, but the body reacts as on the virtual roller coaster ride we discussed above. It doesn't know the difference. We can't do anything to change the past, but we can do something to change the future of our virtual reality. The conscious mind can do this. Neuroscience concludes that our minds are malleable, and this malleability is called neuroplasticity. Neuroscience has only discovered what scripture has declared for thousands of years. "Don't copy the behavior and customs of this world, but let God transform you into a new person by changing the way you think." (Romans 12:2 NLT)

Whether we live in the past or future, we always experience it in the now, concluding that the past, present, and future can all happen simultaneously. We all have this creative nature within us; the only question is, what are we creating? Indeed, we create every time we formulate a thought. It becomes active in our conscious minds. Whether the thought is good or bad, you experience it as if it is happening in the present.

In the grand orchestra of our existence, thoughts are the harmonious melodies that resonate through the chambers of our minds. They are the ethereal creations that spark and dance with the alignment of electrons, the delicate threads of electricity that weave through the tapestry of our consciousness. Like a skilled photographer capturing a fleeting moment, our minds capture these thoughts and transform them into vivid images. They are the photons that illuminate our perception, casting light upon the path we tread. With each passing moment, our video of life unfolds, capturing the essence of who we are and shaping the story we choose to tell.

Deep within the inner sanctum of our being resides the hypothalamus, a wondrous pharmacy of the brain. It holds the key to unlocking the vast spectrum of emotions that color our existence. With its gentle touch, it releases a symphony of chemicals, signifying the emotions that accompany our thoughts. It is the conductor of our emotional orchestra, guiding us through the highs and lows, and reminding us of the beauty of our human experience. And in the intricate dance of our biology, our genes awaken. They are activated, like dormant artists, ready to create masterpieces of proteins. These proteins form the synaptic connections that store this exquisite information, the thoughts that shape our very essence. They are the architects of our neural pathways, the foundation upon which our memories and experiences are built.

Embrace the power of your thoughts. For within them lies the ability to shape your reality, to create a life that resonates with purpose and passion. Each thought is a brushstroke upon the canvas of your existence, an opportunity to paint a world of beauty and inspiration. You are the creator, the artist, and the architect of your thoughts. Embrace this power, for it is within you that the extraordinary resides.

Neuroscience states that long-term conditions of stress or chaos cause disease through negative thoughts alone. If you think about it, you will become it, as time goes on. The amygdala is part of the brain that aids in managing your emotions and helps to recognize threatening stimuli. In fight-or-flight mode, the body releases cortisol, adrenaline, and noradrenaline to know how to react when in danger. It is okay to experience a moment of stress, but not stay in it.

Here is an example of a repressed thought; You are ten years old, going to an amusement park. You're excited and happy. You're with your friends, and you pass by a bus on the way there. This is the best day of your young life, creating joyful memories. You've created those memories, so any time you pass a bus, it will bring back this moment of excitement when you were ten.

On the contrary, creating a bad memory would be passing a bus on the way to an amusement park where you almost drowned. This will become a negative memory that is stored away in your subconscious. When you're fifty years old, going by bus may still invoke fear because of your bad experience at the amusement park. Whenever the memory arises, you remember the same negative feeling from your past. That is the power of thought and memory.

Conscience Birth

The birth of our creative nature, our morality, started in the garden when Adam and Eve took from the Tree of Knowledge of Good and Evil. The tree represented awareness with knowledge. There they received an understanding of what good and evil are, and this awakened their grasp of evil. The voice of God asked, "Who told you that you are naked?" (Genesis 3:11 NIV). The first emotion they experienced after the fall was fear. The second was shame, followed closely by guilt. Isn't this the same process that still unfolds today in our minds every time we stray away from God's best knowledge?

We have all been battling fear ever since the experience in the garden. Our settings have been altered from the beginning. We weren't created to fear but to love. Fear is a learned behavior, and living in fear is not part of the human package. Fear serves us well during temporary danger, but constant fear is not normal. In a jungle, a gazelle can eat grass calmly, but once a threat arises, it will run away in fear. Fear, therefore, serves to preserve the gazelle. But once the danger is no longer present, the gazelle will return to eating grass. How many presumed threats are we still running from by thought alone although the threats are no longer current? Why can't we, as human beings, learn from the gazelle? To shift back to calm.

In the midst of chaos and uncertainty, it is crucial to remember that we are wired for love and peace. Deep within us lies a simple and innocent nature, a nature that craves connection, compassion, kindness, and peace. But as we journey through life, we often find ourselves caught in the clutches of fear.

At the age of twenty-eight, our prefrontal cortex which is located in the front of our brain fully matures and develops giving us the ability to make wiser choices, but that's not the case all the time. It is during this transformative period that we experience the pull of societal expectations and the influence of our surroundings. Our once pure and loving nature can become clouded by the noise of the world.

Yet, even in the face of these challenges, we have the ability to tap into our inner voice, to discern between the angel and the devil perched on our shoulders. We possess the power to choose the path of love and peace, to listen to the whispers of our conscience, and to rise above the negativity that surrounds us. Guarding the door of our thoughts becomes our responsibility. We have the power to filter out negativity, and to choose what enters our minds and hearts. We can choose to focus on the positive, seek inspiration, and surround ourselves with uplifting influences. It may not always be easy but remember that within you lies a wellspring of strength and resilience. You possess the capacity to overcome adversity and transform fear into love and peace. Embrace the power of choice and let your actions be guided by compassion, empathy, and kindness.

Between our eyes is the pineal gland and the frontal lobe is behind the forehead. This is the door or gate to our minds. Guarding our minds above all else starts here—between our two eyes and being aware of our thoughts. What are we allowing to be created in our thoughts? The brain is like an assembly plant; it just creates. It does not reject the bad in favor of the good; it just does its job - collecting and storing data. Our job is to discern what is good and bad. Again Combining thoughts, energy, and focused attention produces mental real estate in your brain. A synaptic connection then forms where the thought is created. The invisible becomes visible. Isn't that amazing? Just like God, we were made to create.

Mental Hardware

God has given us the ability to create our world within the unseen realm of our minds so that we get to see it in our minds before we see it in the natural world. This ability is truly spectacular! We are created with the power to do everything our childlike hearts can imagine and bring it forth into the world through our actions.

I remember when I was about eight years old, I had dreams. I would close my eyes and design where I wanted to go and what I wanted to do. This should be our norm. To be creative is our nature. To create from the unseen is a trait from the Creator, imparted to us to continue to create our world. This skill is innate, and we can never lose it. It's the God-like character that fuels our hope!

God created us in his image and likeness. (See Genesis 1:26 NIV.) Think about the word "image." "Image" implies that we were an idea in God's mind, an image before he created us! "Likeness" means that, as God created the best world possible, we, too, can create the best world for us. We're designed to build, grow, and flourish. He gave us this remarkable tool called consciousness. This God-given ability gives us the capacity to create, just like God.

I want to reiterate that our minds are our canvases. Robin Sharma, author of the 5 a.m. club states everything is created twice, once in your mind and then in reality. We design, create, and dream what we want and design it in the unseen first; only then do we manifest it in the conscious realm. This can be the best tool for life, but what happens when that stops? What happens when adults no longer have childlike dreams? Do we feel and accept that this is the deck of cards handed to us? Where does hope go? What happens with our goals and hopes? Does reality overcome hope?

Just as we can create a brilliant world, opposing forces are at hand, fighting for our canvases. They want to control your paintbrush. Whoever has your paintbrush is the one who will control the narrative of your life. This is why it's so important to be self-aware. Neuroscience says we have over sixty thousand thoughts a day. Of those sixty thousand thoughts, only 9 percent are new, and 91 percent surface from our subconscious minds. A staggering 70 percent of the 91 percent is negative. This is a powerful statement because where our focus rests, this will grow, whether good or bad. What happens next? The invisible becomes visible. I want you to grasp this and accept that you are the Creator of your future. It starts in your mind. We create today, right now, for the future. What is it going to look like?

Awareness

A famous saying has been going around "Stay woke!" It also appears in the forms "He's woke," "She's woke," and "We all woke." You get the idea. "Woke" refers to a birth of self-awareness, which wasn't there before. It's the ability to think outside your thinking! We have the God-given ability to come outside our thoughts and look at what we're thinking. It's called multiple-perspective advantage (MPA).

The term MPA was coined by one of my best friends, Caroline Leaf. (Even though I haven't met her, she's my friend.) MPA is a unique God-given ability to observe what we are observing. We have been given this as a tool to ensure that what we create is the right future. We have the power to choose between positive and negative thoughts by observing what we keep on thinking about, and choosing what to think about and what to cast down.

Just like the plus sign, positive thoughts have the remarkable ability to add value to our lives. They uplift us, inspire us, and propel us forward on our journey. Positive thoughts create a harmonious balance in our minds, filling us with hope, optimism, and a sense of possibility. They remind us that every problem has a solution, every setback is an opportunity in disguise, and every failure is a stepping stone towards success.

On the other hand, negative thoughts, represented by the negative sign, act as a constant subtractor. They have the power to take away joy, motivation, and confidence from our lives. Negative thoughts can cloud our judgment, hinder our progress, and prevent us from reaching our full potential. They drain our energy and leave us feeling stuck and discouraged.

Negative thoughts steal your energy and hinder your progress. It's important to understand that these negative thoughts thrive when they are given attention and fed with our precious energy. Imagine starting your day with a full tank of energy, but then allowing 40 percent of it to be drained by these negative issues immediately in the morning. Suddenly, you find yourself with only 60 percent of your energy remaining. It's no wonder that exhaustion starts to creep in, weighing you down like extra luggage. But fear not, for there is a way to overcome this spiritual exhaustion. We will go into more depth regarding this later but for now, it begins with awareness of these negative thoughts and choosing what we give our attention to.

In the vast realm of our minds, our thoughts hold incredible power. Being aware of them is a superpower. They shape our perspective, influence our emotions, and guide our actions. It is both fascinating and daunting to consider the impact our thoughts can have on our well-being. Psychologists have shed light on an intriguing concept: the notion that our subconscious mind, often referred to as our second brain, plays a significant role in our mental health. They propose that once a staggering 65 percent of our thought lives are consumed by negativity, we may find ourselves grappling with clinical depression.

While this statistic may initially sound alarming, it serves as a powerful reminder of the importance of cultivating a positive mindset and being aware of our thought lives. We hold within us the ability to shape our thoughts, to consciously choose the narratives that play out in our minds. It is through this conscious effort and awareness that we can create a shift, transforming our thought patterns and ultimately improving our overall well-being. Remember that every thought we entertain has the potential to shape our reality. By consciously redirecting our thinking towards positivity, we can unlock a world of possibilities. We become architects of our happiness, constructing a foundation built on optimism and resilience.

It is our responsibility to create the life we want to live. We can never give it to somebody else because God has given responsibility uniquely to every person. We can allow all the positive thoughts in our minds and cast down all negative thoughts.

"The weapons we fight with are not the weapons of the world. On the contrary, they have the divine power to demolish strongholds. We demolish arguments and every pretension that sets itself up against the knowledge of God, and we take captive every thought to make it obedient to Christ" (2 Corinthians 10:4–5 NIV).

Birth of Identity

The birth or concept of ego is the conscience and sub-conscience mind working together to protect yourself. The ego is often associated with our sense of self and how we identify ourselves. It can be seen as a protective system or defense mechanism that we develop over time. Especially in our early years of life. Unfortunately, these protective mechanisms, which initially shield us from pain and hurt, can eventually hinder our growth and development in society.

These protective measures, fueled by our past experiences of pain, hurt, and trauma, become like a shield that we hide behind. They shape our perception of ourselves and influence how we interact with the world. We may become so accustomed to these protective mechanisms that they become our permanent identity, and we unconsciously allow them to control our lives.

This understanding was a game changer for me having the understanding of MPA officially known as meta-cognition which is the ability to look at self from the outside. This allows us the ability to see the faulty programs that we have instilled over the years in our lives. I saw clearly when my ego was operating within me and this transformed my awareness forever and started my change to my original setting. Once you know something you can't ignore it any longer. In my studies, I also learned about another concept called superego. The superego is passed down from your parents, environment, and culture as early as five years old. This keen awareness is a game changer that created a new version of myself because I acknowledged my ego and superego changing the narrative of what was. I was able to unravel myself from my 8-year-old version to my current age.

Ego reminds me of an old movie "The Wizard of Oz," where the character of Oz projected an image of fearlessness and power to the people, making them believe he was someone to be feared. In reality, this projection was nothing more than a protective measure to hide his deep-seated insecurities. Just like Oz, our ego often masks our true selves with a façade of strength and confidence. It creates a persona that we present to the world, a carefully constructed image that we hope will be accepted and admired. We strive to be seen as fearless, powerful, and in control, all while hiding our vulnerabilities and fears.

The ego, driven by the fuel of pain and trauma, may develop a distorted way of thinking. The problem lies in accepting the ego's narrative as truth, when in fact, it is based on lies and distortions rooted in our past hurts and traumas. In a spiritual context, when Jesus says, "Let him deny himself, take up his cross, and follow me," (Matthew 16:24 ESV) He is essentially urging us to let go of our ego and our self-centered ways. It is an invitation to surrender our false identity built upon pain and trauma in our thoughts, and instead, embrace our true selves. This process involves dying to our ego, shedding the protective mechanisms that hinder our growth, and reconnecting with our original, authentic selves.

By recognizing the influence of our ego and understanding its limitations, we can begin the journey towards self-discovery and personal growth to return to our original settings, not the distorted ones. It requires a willingness to let go of the false narratives and beliefs that the ego has constructed, and instead, embrace a more authentic way of being. In my studies, I have learned that ego is in the mind but a close relative to ego is pride which is in the heart. Pride is thinking too high or too low of yourself. Like a quarter has two sides and both have the same value so is pride. It is taking on the identity of your altered version and making it certain. In other words, you believe it to be true in mind and heart. "For as he thinks in his heart, so is he." (Proverbs 23:7 NKJV) When we take on this identity in our hearts this unauthentic self is what God opposes. As stated in James 4:6 (NKJV) "God resists the proud, But gives grace to the humble." Now I can understand why God opposes the proud, not only are we destroying ourselves but also destroying people which is God's heart. This awareness of ego and pride is the first step for change to return to our original settings. The process of inner transformation allows us to align with our true essence and live a more fulfilling and purposeful life by disengaging from our altered identity.

In conclusion, it is imperative that we take every thought captive and subject them to careful examination. We must determine whether these thoughts originate externally, as a result of influences from the enemy, or internally, stemming from our own ego or superego. By honing our ability to navigate through the intricacies of our thought life, we embark on a transformative journey towards reconnecting with our original settings.

This process of self-reflection and analysis allows us to discern the true nature of our thoughts and disentangle ourselves from altered identities. By consciously questioning the origins and intentions behind our thoughts, we can gain a deeper understanding of ourselves and our motives.

CHAPTER 2

CULTIVATING THE GARDEN OF OUR HEARTS

Our hearts are like gardens; if we're not mindful of what we allow to grow within them, we may end up with a patch of thorns, thistles, and weeds. Over time, these intrusive thoughts and emotions will choke out the goodness we once possessed. God gave us this responsibility. In Genesis 2:15 it states the lord God placed man in the garden of Eden to tend and watch over it. So now our greatest garden is our hearts. If we neglect our inner gardens, we risk withering away and producing no fruit in life. Surviving life with thorns and thistles is not enough; we must tend to the garden of our hearts to create something of value.

As a new homeowner and gardener, I have come to realize that growing green grass is a complex and meticulous process that demands constant attention. As I worked on my garden, I couldn't help but draw parallels between this endeavor and the spiritual realm.

It all starts with the seeds. Just like when we plant positive thoughts in our minds, we have to be careful and intentional about what we allow to take root. However, I soon discovered that the challenges were plentiful. Birds swooped down and devoured the seeds, preventing any grass from sprouting. It reminded me of how external influences can sometimes hinder our positive mindset if we let them.

But it didn't end there. Even if the seeds managed to evade the hungry birds, there was no guarantee that they would grow into lush green grass. And then there are the weeds. They seem to sprout out of nowhere, spreading their roots and stealing the nutrients meant for the grass. Negativity can be just like those pesky weeds, slowly choking our positive thoughts and preventing them from flourishing. Just as I need to be vigilant in pulling out the weeds from my garden, we must be proactive in uprooting negative thoughts from our minds.

Through these experiences, I've come to appreciate the intricate connection between our thoughts and our reality. Our minds, like gardens, require consistent care and attention. It's our responsibility given by God. We must make a conscious effort to intentionally sow positive seeds, protect them from external influences, and weed out negativity. It is truly fascinating how the lessons learned from something as simple as gardening can reveal profound truths about our spiritual and mental well-being.

We often shy away from confronting the negative thoughts that arise when someone offends us. These are weeds we must tend to. Instead of dealing with the issue head-on, we let resentment and bitterness take root in our minds. As time passes, these weeds grow and spread, suffocating any positive emotions that once bloomed in our hearts. When we allow the goodness within us to flow freely, we experience the positive flow of life. However, if we block or poison this flow, it can lead to our destruction. Bitterness, resentment, anger, and unforgiveness are toxins that destroy our hearts if left unchecked. We must cultivate our inner gardens. We need to root out the weeds and nurture the goodness within us. Facing our souls and dealing with negative emotions is essential to our well-being. By becoming a wellspring of life, we can experience the abundance of life that is available to us. We must be mindful of the thoughts and emotions we allow to grow within us and confront negative feelings head-on. Only by cultivating the goodness within us, can we create abundance around us.

Unfortunately, most of us are not taught how to garden and plant seeds that will produce abundance in our lives. We tend to seek information from our surroundings, which often have a fallen mindset, keeping us growing thorns and thistles. However, through Jesus' precepts, we can change back to our original settings in the heart and no longer have to work for it.

In the realm of botanical wonders, it is intriguing to explore the journey of seeds transforming into fruits. However, before delving into this fascinating process, let us delve into the profound analogy presented by Jesus, comparing his words to seeds. As we engage in deep contemplation of his teachings, we assume the role of diligent farmers, meticulously planting these seeds within the fertile soil of our hearts.

Indeed, merely superficially sowing a seed and hastily covering it with a thin layer of soil would not suffice. Instead, we must summon the conviction to dig deeply, ensuring that the seed is firmly planted. Similarly, our responsibility lies in the act of meditating upon the word of God. The more we immerse ourselves in this practice, the more profound the embedding of the seed within us becomes.

Remarkably, it is crucial to recognize that the word itself possesses an innate ability to germinate and flourish within the depths of our hearts. Consequently, this growth nourishes the development of virtuous and Godly fruits in our lives. The correlation between seeds and fruits becomes evident, as the quality and nature of the seeds we sow determine the kind of fruits we shall reap.

Therefore, if our aspiration is to harvest a bountiful yield of Godly fruits, we must diligently and intentionally plant the seeds of God's word. By doing so, we foster an environment where righteousness, compassion, and wisdom can flourish, ultimately enriching our lives and positively impacting those around us.

We must embrace our role as conscientious cultivators, meticulously planting the seeds of divine wisdom within the soil of our hearts. With unwavering commitment and diligent cultivation, we can nurture the growth of Godly fruits.

Fruits

The Bible teaches us that we can identify a person's character by the way they act. "By their fruit you will recognize them. Do people pick grapes from thorn bushes or figs from thistles?" (Matthew 7:16 NIV). But to change external conditions, we must first change internally. This requires us to be open to doing the internal work necessary to bring about the desired change.

Jesus emphasized the importance of remaining in Him to bear fruit. Just like a branch that remains connected to a tree, producing fruit effortlessly due to the flow of sap through its veins, Jesus sought heart transformation rather than mere behavior modification. Joseph Prince said, "Right believing leads to right living."

In contrast, Moses wrote about the curse brought upon man due to disobedience, where he will struggle to make a living as the ground will grow thorns and thistles instead of fruit-bearing crops. These thorns and thistles represent negative thoughts that don't produce life, as they are not natural fruits. They come from the gardens of our hearts and reveal the fruitfulness or fruitlessness of our inner selves, impacting our spiritual lives.

The Truth about Being Doubtful

A documentary on ships at sea inspired me to realize that every person on board has a unique role to play, yet they must work together harmoniously to reach their destination. Similarly, in the spiritual world, the conscious mind and the subconscious mind must come into agreement with truth for it to happen in your life. If in my mind I believe something but in my heart there is unbelief nothing happens. The mind and heart have different roles but must work together for faith to operate. If they are not aligned, we will not reach our desired destination.

Double-mindedness is a state of wavering and indecisiveness, marked by insincerity and hypocrisy. James 1:8 describes this condition as causing instability in all areas of life. Even before science existed, this phenomenon was present in the form of the subconscious and conscious minds. These two minds are always present within us; if they are not in agreement, we remain stagnant and do nothing. However, when our minds are in accordance with our hearts, we can achieve great things.

The term "double-minded" originates from the Greek word "dipsuchos," meaning a person with two minds or souls. This dual mindset leads to opposing forces that hinder progress and stability. Those who struggle with double-mindedness have divided loyalty between God and the world, causing instability in everything they do. (James 1:8 NLT) The problem lies in not allowing the seed to germinate in our hearts and the seed only remains in our minds. Therefore we believe one thing with our minds and our hearts believe another.

Doubt is an internal problem that often results in blaming external factors for our failures. However, the truth is many times we are programmed to fail due to bad programs we receive in our subconscious early in life. I'll explain more thoroughly later in the book. We may want the good God has for us and receive it in our minds, but the programs in our hearts oppose it and reject it. The good news is that we don't have to remain in this state. By aligning our conscious and subconscious or having a mind and heart coherence, we can overcome double-mindedness and succeed.

The Law of Discovery

The Law of Discovery speaks to the importance of exploring our inner selves and discovering our true potential. The analogy of outer space exploration highlights the irony that we often neglect our infinite internal space, which holds limitless possibilities. When was the last time you discovered new planets within yourself? Are you an alien in your own inner world?

I emphasize the existence of two minds - the conscious mind, everything we see with our eyes, and the subconscious mind, where we visualize and our library of life exists. These two minds shape our perception and reaction to things in the world around us.

The message is clear when we take the time to explore our inner selves, we unlock a world of possibilities. I am drawn to the US Army's slogan, "Be all you can be," emphasizing that we, too, can achieve our full potential in God's army, but it all starts within ourselves.

The reference to John 3:16 is used to illustrate the depth of God's love for us and how our internal world is the object of his love in our hearts. By tapping into this love and operating in the fullness of who we are, I suggest we should discover a new world within ourselves so we can be able to achieve great things.

If we want to move toward God, we must change our hearts' settings. Our subconscious mind is the driving force in our lives, and after the fall of Adam, all of humanity went astray because our settings were altered to follow our desires. For instance, when using a GPS app, we enter the destination we want to go to, and the program formulates a route, providing clear instructions that lead us to the intended destination. Similarly, to reach a new destination, we must update our hearts with new information, as our hearts are the ones leading us. However, if we continue to have the same old information in our hearts, we'll go around in circles, failing to reach our desired destination. We must give our hearts new and updated information to become a new version of ourselves.

Adults are naturally adventurous and love discovering new things, just like children. We continue on this quest as we grow up, but often, we don't realize that the most significant discoveries we can make are within our hearts. Jesus says that the kingdom of God is within us. He empowers us to subdue and take back what's ours. Inside us lies a world with limitless potential to attain everything that God intends for us to have.

Matthew 11:12 teaches us that we must take the kingdom of God by force. We need to examine our hearts to see change because change begins from within and spills over into our outer world. In the Garden of Eden, God instructed Adam to subdue the garden, which means to take it. However, this also implies that someone else had taken it over before. While we understand the natural meaning of God's word, we must first capture its spiritual meaning.

God's word has duality, and we must understand it in its duality. These instructions still apply to us today, and we are called to subdue the world within us because someone else has taken it over since Adam's fall. The enemy has been advancing darkness in humanity, and his job is to take over the kingdom of God, which is within us.

Our heart is what the Father in Heaven values the most. We are subdued whenever we give the enemy an open door to our lives. In Puerto Rico, there is a place called La Perla that the government does not have control over it because it was subdued by violent crime families, and now they govern it. Similarly, there are areas of our lives that we do not govern, which we must subdue.

Since the fall of Adam, the enemy has been advancing into our kingdom, and Jesus redeems what the first Adam lost. Therefore, it's time to advance and take over our world and allow it to produce the fruits of God in our lives. In Romans 5:15-18, we see that by Jesus' death and resurrection, we all receive the free gift of grace, forgiveness, and righteousness.

"Yes, Adam's one sin brings condemnation for everyone, but Christ's one act of righteousness brings a right relationship with God and new life for everyone." (Romans 5:18 NLT)

Our thoughts determine our beliefs and our beliefs shape our reality. Therefore, focusing on positive thoughts according to God's word and envisioning a positive future is crucial in our inner world.

The power of our thoughts and the importance of having a clear vision of our inner world is crucial. The Bible warns that without vision, people perish. Without a vision, we can quickly become lost and unfocused. It is essential to have a God-sized vision for our lives and not settle for temporary fixes with which the enemy deceives us.

Let's think of Eve in the Garden of Eden as a metaphor for our inner world. When negative words and doubt enter our inner world it is stripped from its original setting as God intended. It seeks quick fixes that may feel good in the short term but can have long-term adverse effects. Therefore, having a clear vision of our inner world and focusing on positive thoughts according to God's word will shape our beliefs and reality and change our perspectives.

This concept is reinforced in 2 Peter 1:3-4 (ESV), where it is stated that God has granted us everything necessary for life and godliness, including the ability to partake in the divine nature. "His divine power has granted to us all things that pertain to life and godliness, through the knowledge of him who called us to his own glory and excellence, by which he has granted to us his precious and very great promises, so that through them you may become partakers of the divine nature, having escaped from the corruption that is in the world because of sinful desire."

In Proverbs 23:7 (NASB), King Solomon declares that "as he thinks within himself, so he is." Our thoughts and beliefs according to God's word have a powerful impact on our lives, and we can use our creative nature to bring about positive change. To do this, we must nurture our creative abilities and believe in our potential to create our desired reality. By aligning our thoughts and beliefs according to God's word with our goals, we can plant the seeds of change in our hearts and watch them grow. The worst-case scenarios we imagine can become a self-fulfilling prophecy, but by reversing this negative pattern, we can transform our future.

I'll share this last analogy of how the garden of thoughts and the computer are similar. Just like how the words we type on a keyboard appear on the screen, our thoughts manifest in our awareness. However, our thoughts are transient and fleeting. Once the computer is shut down, the words on the screen disappear, just as our thoughts vanish when we divert our attention elsewhere. Unless we intentionally save our thoughts and memorize the information it will be lost.

To preserve our thoughts, we can liken downloading them as a program into the hard drive. This process involves consciously storing our thoughts and memories in our subconscious by meditating day and night. By doing so, our thoughts become part of our internal memory, ensuring that they are retained even after our immediate awareness of them fades.

Similar to how a computer relies on its hard drive to retrieve previously stored information, we can retrieve our thoughts from our memory. By downloading our thoughts into the "hard drive" of our subconscious mind, we can access them whenever we need to recall specific information or reflect on past experiences.

In essence, the process of consciously saving our thoughts is akin to downloading them into our mental storage system. Once saved, our thoughts remain accessible, even when they are no longer at the forefront of our consciousness. This ability to retain and retrieve our thoughts allows us to build upon our knowledge, learn from past experiences, and shape our understanding of the world around us.

So, let us consider the importance of effectively storing our thoughts. By treating our minds as metaphorical hard drives, we can ensure that our valuable ideas and insights are not lost to the passage of time. Let us actively engage in the process of downloading our thoughts, so that they may be readily available to us whenever we need them.

In conclusion, God has given us the gift of imagination and creation to plant the right seeds and by using this gift, we can shape our lives according to our desires. Planting a beautiful garden that produces life. By aligning our thoughts and beliefs with God's word, the seed, and our goals, we can bring about positive change to see God's word fulfilled in our lives producing fruits and becoming partakers of the divine nature. Let us begin to create the best-looking garden possible.

CHAPTER 3

THE INNER WORLDS

Lord, you know everything there is to know about me. You perceive every movement of my heart and soul, and you understand every thought before it even enters my mind. You are so intimately aware of me, Lord. You read my heart like an open book and you know all the words I'm about to speak before I even start a sentence! You know every step I will take before my journey even begins. You've gone into my future to prepare the way, and in kindness, you follow behind me to spare me from the harm of my past. With your hand of love upon my life, you impart a blessing to me. This is just too wonderful, deep, and incomprehensible! Your understanding of me brings me wonder and strength.
—Psalm 139:1–7 (TPT)

In our life's journey, we all want to know where all our perceptions come from and how these perceptions affect our personalities. Where did they originate? In this chapter, we will be trying to answer the following questions:

- Why do I perceive things from a certain point of view?
- Why do I think the way I think?
- Why is my personality the way it is?
- Am I this way because God made me this way, or is this how society molded me?

As you dive into this chapter, you will see that we are products of our environment. The psychological debate of nature vs. nurture is not what I'm necessarily referring to. I am referring to our current habits and perceptions, which have very little to do, at times, with DNA and our genetic pool and more to do with the events that have transpired in our lives. The good news is that we can change this and have the power to recreate who we are. In her book "Switch on Your Brain", Dr. Caroline Leaf states, "But now scientists know that the brain can reorganize throughout life, changing its structure and function through mental experience alone. If the brain can get worse by constantly focusing on the problem, then the brain can get better by understanding how to eliminate and replace the problem." As I have said and will continue to say throughout the book, science is catching up to God!

It's time for us to learn how we can change our future. Most of us may believe that everything that has happened in our lives is based on decisions that we have made. While this is true, what if I told you that the source from which you came up with these perceptions of decisions wasn't entirely based on your doings? You are about to see what makes us perceive the way we do. Is it our parents or is it our own perception? Is it what we see on TV? In movies? This is important because if we can get to the root or origin of this, we can do something about it.

Imagine trying to cut down a tree by cutting off its branches. We all know that it can grow and eventually bear fruit again. However, if we don't want to see the tree bear fruit, we must do one thing: dig it up and pull its roots from the ground! We must attack it at its origins. I'm the first to admit that this is a little more challenging and takes a little more time, but the only way to eliminate the tree entirely is to pull its roots from the ground.

We often want a magic wand, some hocus-pocus incantation, or a feather to touch our forehead and make every negative experience we've been through go away. But the reality is that we have to "dig up" how we perceive those negative experiences. If we pull the tree's roots, the fruits will fall away. We have the God-given ability to create our future and recreate it through our thoughts. In Proverbs 23:7 (KJV), the Bible teaches, "As a man thinks, so is he." This information forces us to hold ourselves accountable and takes away the blame game. After this, we will have the ability and power to change the outcomes of our lives and influence those around us.

Things that remain in the dark, tend to have power over us but we are about to discuss how to regain our power! Please pay close attention; I will be more technical here than in previous chapters. I will discuss the nature of the two parts of the mind in more in-depth and explain why we sometimes have trouble controlling our thought lives. The function of the brain is to perceive signals and interpret them.

To begin, there are signals from the environment that are external. The brain receives this information to determine the necessary response. For example, suppose you are presented with the stimulus of a bear. In that case, your brain receives that information and communicates it to the body to release specific hormones to elicit specific behaviors. In this scenario, the body releases adrenaline to produce a "fight or flight" response.

There are also internal signals by thought alone that activate certain chemicals. Have you ever heard of a study called the placebo effect? It's randomized, double-blinded controlled trials. The placebo effect occurs when you have a very positive thought that some medication can heal you. Even if that medication is a sugar pill, the placebo effect by thought alone can cause you to be healed by it by activating chemicals in the brain to heal you. A drug might not cure us, but our thoughts about the effects of the medication possibly can. Studies conducted over time have shown that the placebo effect holds much merit. However, another effect, the "nocebo effect," highlights how negative thinking can result in a negative outcome after hearing a bad diagnosis from the doctor.

I want to stress this point by stating that negative thinking can exacerbate many side effects of the disease. While the placebo effect can heal you, the nocebo effect, caused by negative thinking, can harm you. Both have the same power to affect your health by thought alone. The power of the mind.

I have used this example before but it is worth mentioning again. I want to compare this to virtual reality (VR). In VR, the mind doesn't know the difference between reality and virtual reality but goes where you want to take it. Most of us figuratively live our lives with virtual reality glasses on. Once you put them on, your perception of truth is what you see.

We know what we perceive is inaccurate, but our minds don't distinguish the difference. The glasses make you feel like you're in another place, possibly at another time. The mind doesn't know the difference; therefore, it releases the same chemicals and toxins as if you are in the place the VR glasses are making you think you are in. I recently saw videos online of people wearing VR glasses running into walls and even falling.

Here is a case scenario: Your mind acts like it's in a place and time other than its present existence (virtual reality). It even releases matching chemicals to make the experience authentic. Even though it all happened in your mind, your mind doesn't know the difference. Your brain responds to what you see and holds true. This is the power of our creative nature.

When you believe your doctor or Google labeling your symptoms, saying you have this or that, you can continue to experience the symptoms by thought alone - even if you don't have that disease.

The medical field has found these truths concerning the power of the mind only in the last few decades. So, belief has become an essential part of medicine, proven true by science. If you believe something is good, it can be good for you. If you think it's harmful to you, it can be detrimental. It's a fantastic time to be alive as medicine, science, and God come together for some much-needed answers. And knowing the power we possess in our minds.

I want to share my experience with the effects of this truth. I remember, when I was the age of ten, my stepfather would come in at three in the morning and declare words over my life. I didn't understand why he would spew such atrocities towards me. He spoke negative words every day, and as time passed, some of the words he spoke over my life came to be. One thing he said was that I would never achieve anything. Another was that I would be a drug user."

By the age of fifteen, I was a drug addict who was not working and was panhandling. I lived in an empty building. Early on in my life, I noticed that if those negative words could come to pass, I could also make the opposite true. At age twenty-five, I was free of drugs and on my way to a career as a self-made businessman who was successful in every way.

I now understand that at that time, my subconscious was recording everything my father was saying, taking it in as truth and therefore manifesting it later in life. That's what happens to the words in our subconscious minds. The subconscious becomes a magnet to attract what you believe to be true. Irrational emotions stem from recorded comments in your subconscious, which, for the purpose of this book, we are going to use the subconscious to symbolize the heart. This is the problem, we often try to modify our behavior, but it doesn't work in the long run. Instead, we should target the area of concern and reprogram our behavior. This is why the apostle Paul says, "Be transformed by the renewal of your mind, that by testing you may discern what is the will of God, what is good and acceptable and perfect" (Romans 12:2 ESV).

The conscious mind is the gatekeeper of the subconscious mind. Let me explain this with an example. In ancient times, some towns were built with protective walls. The employee at the entrance was called a gatekeeper. His job was to work all night and day, watching out for the enemy. When he saw them engage. He will alert everyone of danger. He protects everyone by using fire or bullets to deter the enemy. This is similar to our minds and subconscious minds. The mind is where we are aware of what's happening, and when there's a negative word or thought, we have the power to send a flame or bullet to keep it away! The enemy's negative thoughts want to enter your fortress to destroy you from the inside. He wants to enter your mind and get access to your heart. We see this battle continuing every day. It may seem impossible and complex, but here is a spiritual truth: it gets easier with practice. The writer of Hebrews says it this way: but strong meat belongeth to them that are full of age, even those who by reason of use have their senses exercised to discern both good and evil. (Hebrews 5:14 KJV). He mentions senses as in our five senses (our reasoning) and exercises as something we do daily. This truth can change your life and the generation to follow. I wish someone had taught me this early in life, but now I get to share it with you.

The Sources of Our Perception

Genetics

The development of specific characteristics as we grow up is a fascinating area of study that sheds light on the intricate play between genetics and our environment. It is widely acknowledged that our genes, the biological blueprints inherited from our parents, play a significant role in shaping who we are. These genetic instructions are present in every cell of our bodies, and they provide the foundation upon which our individual traits are built.

From the moment of conception, our genes set the stage for our development. They determine our physical attributes, such as our eye color, hair type, and height. However, genes also influence aspects of our personality, intelligence, and even susceptibility to certain diseases. This complex interplay between genetics and environment is known as nature versus nurture, and it has long been a topic of interest for scientists and researchers.

As we navigate through life, we are influenced by both our genetic predispositions and the environment in which we grow and learn. Our parents, who themselves possess a unique combination of genetic traits, unknowingly pass down these characteristics to us. It is through this process that we inherit certain traits that resemble those of our parents, even if we were not raised alongside them.

Take, for instance, the scenario of a child being raised primarily by their mother, while their father is not present for a significant portion of their early years. Despite the limited exposure to the father, the mother often remarks that the child possesses traits that remind her of the father. This seemingly paradoxical situation can be attributed to the way genes are inherited and expressed.

Genes can be dominant or recessive, meaning that some traits are more likely to be expressed than others. When a child inherits a dominant gene from one parent, it is more likely to be expressed in their physical or behavioral characteristics. In the case mentioned above, it is possible that the child inherited certain dominant genes from the father, resulting in similarities that the mother observed.

Furthermore, genes can interact with each other and with the environment in complex ways, further shaping our development. The field of epigenetics explores how external factors, such as diet, stress, and exposure to toxins, can modify gene expression. These modifications can occur throughout our lives, and they can influence our physical and mental well-being.

Understanding the role of genetics in our development has far-reaching implications. It can help us comprehend why certain traits run in families, why some individuals are more susceptible to certain diseases, and even guide medical interventions and personalized treatments.

Moreover, acknowledging the influence of genetics can foster empathy and compassion, as it highlights the unique individuality of each person's genetic makeup.

Our genetic makeup plays a significant role in our development. The traits we inherit from our parents are wired into our original settings and contribute to the individuals we become. While the environment also shapes us, our genes provide the foundation upon which our characteristics are built. Recognizing and understanding the influence of genetics can lead to a deeper appreciation for the complexity of human development and pave the way for further discoveries in the field of genetics.

Subconscious Mind (Our Library)

Our second source of perception, the subconscious mind, is where our learned habits and experiences are recorded. I like to call these our libraries because it's where all our stories of life are written and stashed away. Keeping this metaphor, our subconscious mind stores our beliefs, values, and traditions as "books." The information, or "stories," recorded in these books come into our conscious minds when we need to access them. These programs are acquired primarily in our first seven years of life, in which we download information from our surroundings to store it in our subconscious. For example, when we are younger, our mind relies heavily on our surroundings to absorb information to transfer and store in our subconscious mind. We learn how to walk in the early stages of life, which is stored in our subconscious mind. Eventually, we don't have to actively think about walking because it becomes second nature since it is stored in our skills library. That ultimately frees our conscious mind to think about other things.

Since we record this information during these early stages of life, we don't always filter between true and false. That is why it is crucial, as we get older, to be aware of our subconscious programs because they may affect our thinking.

The Conscious Mind

The third source of perception is the conscious mind. The conscious mind pertains to creative programming while the subconscious mind pertains to learned habits. When you are aware of negative thought patterns programmed into your subconscious, you can rewrite your perception of your life experiences. You can bring everything back to its original setting and become all that God has created you to be. This is revolutionary! The conscious mind is one of the most powerful things in the world. But many times, we fail to maximize its ability. Many people are unaware of the creative power they have in their conscious minds and that they can, in fact, rewrite and restructure their futures by rewriting what they perceive today.

Brain Development Stages

The following section will explain the five brain development stages and how they relate to our awareness according to Bruce Lipton. Here is a short overview. As we grow and develop, our brain transitions from a Delta state to a Beta state. This progression helps us gain insight into our identity by understanding our early life experiences. Brain waves are electrical patterns that are produced by the synchronized activity of neurons in the brain. These waves can be measured using electroencephalography (EEG) and are categorized into different frequency bands, including Delta, Theta, Alpha, Beta, and Gamma.

Delta waves are the slowest brain waves, ranging from 0.5 to 4 Hz. They are typically observed during deep sleep and are associated with restorative and regenerative processes in the body. As we progress into the Theta state, with frequencies ranging from 4 to 8 Hz, we experience a dream-like state, light sleep, and deep relaxation. Alpha waves, ranging from 8 to 13 Hz, are dominant when we are awake but in a relaxed state with our eyes closed. They are associated with a calm and meditative state of mind. As we become more alert and engaged, our brain transitions into a beta state, which ranges from 13 to 30 Hz. Beta waves are associated with focused attention, problem-solving, and active thinking.

Throughout our early development, our brain states evolve. Infants primarily exhibit Delta and Theta waves, reflecting their need for restorative sleep and exploration of the world. As children grow older, they transition into Alpha and Beta states, allowing for increased cognitive abilities, learning, and social interaction.

Understanding this progression of brain waves can provide valuable insights into our development and sense of self. By reflecting on our early brain states, we can gain a better understanding of how our experiences and environments have shaped us. This knowledge can help us navigate our lives and make informed decisions as we continue to grow and evolve.

1. Delta waves: Are the slowest brain waves associated with deep sleep and unconsciousness.
2. Theta waves: Are typically present during light sleep and are also associated with meditation and deep relaxation.
3. Alpha waves: Are present during wakefulness and relaxation and are associated with a calm and focused state of mind.
4. Beta waves: Are associated with active thinking, problem-solving, and concentration. They are also present during stress and anxiety.
5. Gamma waves: Are the fastest brain waves associated with high-level cognitive processing and consciousness.

Delta Brain State

During the delta brain development state, which encompasses the initial two years of an infant's life, the child typically operates at the lowest frequency, spending a significant amount of time asleep or unaware of their surroundings. Referred to as the delta brain states, this period is characterized by a lack of consciousness and a reliance on absorbing information from the environment.

As human beings, we undergo a substantial learning process during our childhood, acquiring numerous social and familial skills that enable us to integrate into society. However, at this early stage, our innate capabilities do not encompass the ability to create novel concepts or ideas. Instead, our natural predisposition is to indiscriminately absorb and assimilate data.

It is during this phase that children demonstrate an exceptional capacity for rapid and extensive learning, often referred to as super or hyper-learning. Remarkably, children at this age can effortlessly acquire proficiency in multiple languages simultaneously, showcasing their remarkable adaptability and ability to absorb new information within seconds.

The delta state is a critical period in a child's development, laying the foundation for future learning and growth. It is through the exploration and assimilation of knowledge during this phase that infants begin to shape their understanding of the world around them and acquire the necessary skills to navigate and thrive in their social and cultural environments.

I remember speaking to a person that I was counseling. In that counseling session, he remembered his mother choking and drowning him. It was so powerful and emotional that he started crying while talking about it. The trauma was recorded in his subconscious, but he didn't know it. This was a thirty-three-year-old memory from a state where most don't remember anything. The delta state is a part of us that we're not aware of but that we know is recording everything. A powerful perception of his mother that was etched inside his subconscious. Whenever someone said to him, "mother," this was the lens through which he perceived his mother.

Everything we hear, see, smell, or experience from the womb until we are about six years old, goes straight into our subconscious as a recording. All we do during that time is become precise recorders of all information, whether good or bad. Some habits and thoughts are based on subconscious recordings of our parents, family, friends, culture, TV, and other media. They all contributed to who we became. No one asked us whether we wanted to download this information. We didn't have a say-so in the environment that we grew up in. These programs that were downloaded into our lives ultimately created and shaped the person we came to be.

If you are having a child or are a parent, be cautious of your words. The next chapter focuses on the creative nature of words. Comments can be recorded even in children's subconscious minds in the womb. In the first six years of a child's life, their mind is programmable. It is characterized by a malleable mind susceptible to recording specific information.

At the inner healing school I attended in Alaska the instructors discussed profound traumas we may experience. They said that even in the third trimester, while in the womb, a baby records its surroundings. One of the teachers told us a true story about what we had just studied. In Alaska, it is common for people to have heated blankets. When this young mother was nine months pregnant, and her heated blanket developed a short and caught on fire, she quickly panicked and removed the blanket and did not use it anymore. Two years later, the mother offered her son a heated blanket. Instantly he went into a panic and wanted the blanket off him. The boy was reacting to a trauma he experienced while in his mother's womb but didn't remember it. His mother instantly realized he was responding to the incident while he was in the womb two years ago.

Theta Brain State

The theta brain state, spanning from the age of two to six, is characterized by a heightened sense of imagination and a blending of the real and fictional worlds during playtime. Children in this state often interact with imaginary friends, a testament to the vividness of their imaginative abilities. These friends become so tangible within their minds that they may even mistake them for real entities.

Furthermore, the theta state is pivotal in terms of cognitive development, as it marks a period of rapid and extensive learning. Children at this age possess an astonishing capacity for absorbing knowledge and acquiring new skills. Their ability to grasp concepts and information surpasses that of any other developmental state. This is evident in their inclination to correct adults when they perceive inaccuracies and their tendency to parrot words and phrases they have heard. It is important to note that this state is colloquially referred to as the "terrible twos," although it often extends beyond the age of two, persisting until around twelve years old.

During the theta state, children's curiosity reaches new heights, propelling their exploration of the world around them. This innate curiosity acts as a driving force, prompting them to question, investigate, and seek understanding. It is through this natural inclination that children gain a deeper understanding of their environment, broadening their knowledge and expanding their cognitive horizons.

I remember my mom giving me a dog when I was six. It was a dachshund. I loved my dog. One day we went to the store, and I put the leash on the dog and tied the leash to a tree. However, when we returned, we saw the leash with no dog. That was a devastating traumatic experience. Even though we put posters up in the neighborhood, we never found the dog again.

Now, later in life, when I look at a dog, I would say, I don't want anything to do with it, while anybody else might look at it and see how cute the puppy is. However, because of the trauma I experienced, during the theta state, I have never wanted a dog again. Now I am older and able to connect the trauma dots and ask myself, "Why am I perceiving that dog in such a way that I don't want to deal with it?" Most people love dogs; after all, the dog is "man's best friend." and after resolving the glitches in my subconscious I was free of the trauma. I'm hoping to buy a new dog soon because my wife wants a dog, and I have been able to unlearn my negative emotions about dogs.

From age six, that single experience of losing my dog shaped my entire perspective on dogs. Like the womb baby, I reacted only to the trauma. I was responding from my subconscious mind to every dog I saw. Now that I am older and understand the principle of the subconscious mind, this trauma loosened its grip on my conscious behaviors. Now I understand that in this state of my life, I was only recording what was happening around me.

Alpha Brain State

During the next seven to thirteen years of our lives, we still exist in a programmed recording state of mind but reasoning allows us to create our own thoughts from programs already downloaded in our lives and our environment. This state greatly influences our beliefs, aspirations, and thoughts in our future life. Understanding the significance of this is crucial. As we develop and lay the foundation for ourselves, experts in the field like Dr. Caroline Leaf emphasize the profound impact that our thoughts and self-perception have on the functioning of our brains. This underscores the importance of comprehending the programming we undergo during this critical state.

It is essential to recognize that during our early years, specifically in the Alpha state, we have no control over what beliefs and values are instilled in us. We are like sponges, absorbing everything that is around us. However, armed with the knowledge of how this programming works, we can embark on a transformative journey that will redefine who we are.

The brain operates in different stages, and during the Alpha state, our brains are highly receptive to external stimuli. This means that the information we encounter during this time has a profound impact on our subconscious mind. Our subconscious mind is responsible for our automatic thoughts, habits, and beliefs, which greatly shape our behavior and choices later in life.

During these programmable recording states, our brains are like a blank canvas waiting to be painted upon. The experiences, interactions, and messages we receive from our environment are imprinted on this canvas, forming the foundation of our belief systems. These beliefs can be positive or negative, empowering or limiting, depending on what we are exposed to during this critical state.

If we grow up in a nurturing and supportive environment, where we are encouraged to explore, learn, and express ourselves, our programming will likely be positive and empowering. However, if we are exposed to negativity, criticism, and limitations, our programming may be filled with self-doubt, fear, and limitations.

The good news is that our brains are not fixed entities. They are highly adaptable and capable of rewiring themselves. This means that even if our early programming was negative or limiting, we can change it. By becoming aware of our thoughts, beliefs, and self-perception, we can consciously reprogram our minds.

Through mentally rehearsing biblical scriptures, positive affirmations, and visualization, we can replace negative beliefs with positive ones. By consistently reinforcing new empowering beliefs, we can create new neural pathways in our brains, rewiring our thinking patterns and behavior.

Understanding the impact of our early programming allows us to take control of our lives and shape our destinies. It empowers us to challenge and change the beliefs that no longer serve us and to cultivate new ones that align with our true potential. So, no matter what our early experiences were, we have the power to break free from the limitations they may have imposed on us. We can consciously choose the beliefs and aspirations that will guide us toward a fulfilling and successful life.

During my formative years, at the tender age of 10, I was introduced to a game that would have a profound impact on my life - Monopoly. Little did I know then, that this seemingly innocuous board game would shape my perception of the world and eventually lead me down a path towards a career in real estate development.

As a child, everything held a certain truth in my eyes, and playing Monopoly became a tangible representation of this belief. The game taught me valuable lessons about property ownership, negotiation, and strategic thinking. It ignited a spark within me, a fascination with the concept of owning and developing real estate.

Fast forward to the age of 18, when I purchased my first property. It was a moment of immense pride and accomplishment, validating the seeds that had been planted all those years ago. The experience of becoming a property owner only further solidified my passion for the world of real estate.

From that point on, I immersed myself in the realm of property development. I sought out knowledge, honed my skills, and leveraged every opportunity to expand my understanding of this dynamic industry. Each project undertaken became a testament to the influence Monopoly had on my life, propelling me forward with unwavering determination.

Looking back, it is clear that Monopoly served as a catalyst for my journey into the world of real estate. It opened my eyes to the immense potential that lies within properties, instilling in me a desire to create, innovate, and transform spaces. It gave me the confidence to navigate the complexities of the market, and the resilience to overcome challenges along the way.

Understanding this process is the key to unlocking our true potential and living a life aligned with our original settings. By comprehending the relationship between our thoughts, self-perception, and brain function, we gain the power to shape our own destinies. This section of the book holds transformative insights that can empower us to break free from the limitations imposed by our early programming and create a life that is in harmony with our deepest desires.

It is my intention to provide you with a professional and informative discourse on this subject matter. By delving into the science behind our programming and offering practical strategies for self-redefinition, I aim to equip you with the tools necessary to embark on this transformative journey.

Beta Brain State

The beta state encompasses the crucial period between ages thirteen and twenty-eight, during which individuals embark on a journey of self-discovery and self-identity formation. This state, commonly referred to as adolescence, is often associated with the concept of an "identity crisis," and for valid reasons.

Adolescence serves as a critical juncture for individuals to establish a clear sense of self. Those who can successfully navigate this state and develop a distinct self-identity tend to possess stronger goals and a deeper understanding of themselves than their peers who struggle to break free from the influences of their parents or friends. It is important to note that adolescents who excessively rely on their parents for social interaction and guidance may face difficulties in achieving this crucial step towards self-identity.

During this transformative period, individuals are driven to explore various aspects of their personality, interests, values, and beliefs. They may experiment with different roles and behaviors, questioning societal norms and seeking their own unique path. This process of self-discovery often involves grappling with conflicting emotions, navigating through complex relationships, and making important life choices.

Adolescents who successfully emerge from this state with a strong sense of self are more likely to exhibit higher levels of self-confidence, autonomy, and resilience. They possess a clearer vision of their aspirations and are better equipped to make informed decisions aligned with their authentic selves.

What parents tell us, we often become. This is one of the most crucial parts because words become building blocks that establish our internal structure for the rest of our lives. The good news is that even if we are removed from our original settings, we can return to them. If a parent tells us that we are smart, bright, intelligent, and super talented, these words become healthy building blocks of our future.

Scripture states that "we should train a child in the way he should go and that when he is old, he will not depart from it" (Proverbs 22:6 NKJV). When I became a dad I was unconsciously implementing positive programs in his mind. My oldest son is named Sergio, but as a child, I called him Sergenius. Today he is talented in many different fields. This is partly because I trained his subconscious positively; this was rooted in his heart.

"If we fail to train, we will fail to see results." In Jewish custom, they teach the Torah to children as young as four to maturity. The values children learn from you will be with them for life. At an early age they are taught God's Word so that when the conscious mind comes into play during the beta state, they can make sound decisions because the Word of God gives them the wisdom to make Godly choices and know the difference. This builds a foundation for them as they navigate through the beta state.

When it comes to investment properties, one of the most crucial aspects to consider is the foundation. While exterior and interior aesthetics may be appealing, it is imperative to prioritize the structural integrity of the foundation. This principle holds true not only in the realm of real estate but also in our personal lives.

Similar to a cracked foundation in a property, our lives can crumble under the weight of external pressures if our own foundation is compromised. Regrettably, we often find ourselves in this situation without any control over the initial crack in our foundation. It is disheartening to realize that this flaw has been ingrained within us from the start, leading to the subsequent deterioration of everything we build. It is essential to resist the inclination to play the blame game in such circumstances. Instead, we must embrace this insight and utilize it to our advantage. By acknowledging the existence of this crack, we can take proactive measures to reinforce and fortify our foundation.

Disempowering negative programs that have been downloaded into our minds over the years is beneficial. These programs are the result of negative beliefs, past traumas, societal conditioning, and self-doubt. These disempowering programs can manifest in various ways. They can hold us back from pursuing our dreams, hinder our personal growth, and prevent us from living up to our true potential. They create cracks in our foundation, weakening our ability to sustain and achieve our goals.

The first step towards repairing our foundation is recognition. We must become aware of these disempowering programs that are running in our minds. This requires introspection, self-reflection, and a willingness to face our fears and insecurities head-on. Once we have identified these disempowering programs, we can begin the process of fixing them. This involves challenging our negative beliefs, reframing our perspectives, and replacing self-doubt with self-confidence. It requires a commitment to personal growth, self-care, and continuous learning.

Repairing our foundation is not an easy task. It requires dedication, patience, and resilience. Just like fixing a broken house, it may involve tearing down old structures, rebuilding from scratch, and reinforcing weak areas. But the end result is worth it - a solid foundation that can support the weight of our dreams and aspirations. With a strong foundation, we can navigate through life with confidence and clarity. We can pursue our passions, overcome challenges, and live a purposeful life. We become unstoppable forces, capable of achieving anything we set our minds to.

Gamma State

The gamma state of brain activity is characterized by the presence of high-frequency gamma brainwaves. These brainwaves facilitate the simultaneous processing of information from different areas of the brain, allowing for rapid and efficient communication between neural networks. To access gamma frequencies, one must be in a meditative state, as these brainwaves are the subtlest among the various brainwave frequencies.

In the gamma stage, the brain operates at its highest level of awareness and consciousness. It combines the frequencies of beta, alpha, theta, and delta waves, merging them into a harmonious blend of cognitive activity. This unique state of brainwave activity enables us to delve into the deeper realms of our consciousness and modify our perceptions.

One of the significant aspects of gamma waves is that they operate beneath the threshold of our conscious awareness. The programs that drive our thoughts, emotions, and behaviors are often stored in the subconscious mind. By accessing and observing these programs in the gamma stage, we can gain insight into the underlying factors that shape our perception of the world.

The ability to modify these subconscious programs is key to transforming our perspective and altering the way we perceive reality. By recognizing and understanding the patterns and beliefs that drive our thoughts and actions, we can consciously choose to reprogram them, thereby reshaping our perception of the world around us.

It is important to note that this process occurs below the surface of our conscious mind. Our perception of the world is not solely based on what we see, but on the complex interplay of subconscious patterns and beliefs. By actively engaging with the gamma stage and accessing the deeper layers of our consciousness, we can bring about profound shifts in our perception and ultimately change the way we experience life.

The gamma stage represents a state of heightened awareness and cognitive processing. It allows us to access the depths of our subconscious mind, where we can observe and modify the programs that shape our perception of the world. By harnessing the power of gamma brainwaves, we can unlock new possibilities for personal growth, transformation, and a more profound understanding of our existence.

So, let this book be your guide on the journey to repairing your foundation. Let it empower you to recognize the cracks, navigate through the challenges, and rebuild a solid base. Remember, God's big purpose for your life can only be fulfilled when you have a foundation strong enough to sustain it.

CHAPTER 4

THE INCEPTION OF SELF

"Car." "Airplane." "Ship." "Electricity." "Phone." "Computer." "Television." Every word just mentioned is just that—a word. What makes these words essential to us is what they represent. But it wasn't always that way. There was a time when everything mentioned above was simply a thought. Think about this for a second. What if none of these thoughts became ideas that, in time, became concepts that became words that became things that today we are almost dependent on?

What if Martin Luther King's "I Have a Dream" speech was never spoken? What if John F. Kennedy never said, "Don't ask what your country can do for you, but what you can do for your country?" These two speeches alone demonstrate the power of words. They caused shifts to happen in nations. Words can turn us around, but as clearly shown by the two speeches mentioned above, they also have the power to impact the world.

In scripture, we see the value God places on words. He even called his Son the Word! "In the beginning was the Word, and the Word was with God, and the Word was God" (John 1:1 ESV). The scriptures say that all things are created through the Word (Hebrews 11:3 NKJV). We have this creative nature, just like God. According to scripture, all things we see come from the unseen realm and are manifested through words.

Words are Seeds

When we look at a seed, on the outside, all we see is a seed. But every seed has an instruction and an assignment inside. It must accomplish its task here on earth. All we do is plant it and watch it grow. What it needs comes from God, sun, water, and soil.

After reading the first few chapters, you know that our original settings have been altered by words! The Word of God can divide truth and lies like a double-edged sword (Hebrews 4:12 NIV), and we need to believe in His word to counteract the negative words. Whether words are positive or negative, once we believe them to be accurate, they can become part of who we are.

It's easy to see that words have real power. God spoke the world into being by the power of his words. It was God's creative power, and we also have it.

Genesis 12:6 ESV states, "Then God said, "Let us make man in our image, after our likeness. And let them have dominion over the fish of the sea, the birds of the heavens, the livestock, all the earth, and everything that creeps on the earth". Here we read God's nature to create, which he gave us. He made us beings in his likeness, so we harbor creative power, primarily through words.

Words do more than convey information. The power of our words can destroy one's spirit or even stir up hatred and violence. Whoever said, "Sticks and stones may break my bones, but words will never hurt me," needs to be rebuked. (Okay, maybe not rebuked, but just prayed for.)

Words can exacerbate wounds and inflict pain directly. Of all the creatures on this planet, only humans have the ability to communicate through the spoken word. The power to use words is a unique and powerful gift from God. We must ask ourselves, "Are our words healing or hurting ourselves and others?"

"For by your words you will be justified, and by your words, you will be condemned" (Matthew 12:37 NASB). Let's think about that for a second. We often don't realize the power we have. We can convey our thoughts as messages that other humans can understand. We can bring joy or poison or create havoc. We have the uncanny ability to make someone escape from reality. This particular power to verbalize conversations and this avenue to enter other minds is a supernatural power we possess through words.

I was playing volleyball one day, and my team was winning. All the excitement went to my head, and I loudly taunted the other team. While we took a break, the other team got tired of losing, so they stopped playing. We managed to keep the game going, but they had one less person on their team, so, in the spirit of wanting the game to continue, I said I'd go on their team. Immediately, I began encouraging them. We got into a huddle, and I told them how great they were. That motivated everyone and changed the way they looked at the game. We eventually went on to win the next three games! Words shift the perspective of any situation—even volleyball!

We have the undeniable ability to put a smile or a frown on someone's face, the skill to create something, and have it last forever. This can impact people years after our bodies have decomposed and become dust. Our ability to impact each other's lives is a wonderful opportunity that can also be seen as a dreadful responsibility.

Words put together, create, and produce perspective. "Perspective" means "interpretation, spin, belief, conviction, feeling, judgment, mind, mindset, notion, opinion, perception, persuasion, sentiment, verdict, and view." These possibilities are all created by words. They are the building blocks of our original settings. They set the course of all our beliefs at every level, from our values and morals to our characters.

An example of this has to do with our belief systems. They are established very early in our lives. Whatever our parents believe, there's a high probability that we will assume the same things. If they do not believe in God, it usually results in us having no belief in God either. If you had asked me when I was young, "What is your belief system?" I would've said without hesitation, "Catholic." If you had asked why that was my answer, I would've said, "I don't know." I didn't know why I was Catholic, but I knew my mother was, and that is what I was told I was as well. So, it became a part of my programming. In children under twelve, as discussed in the previous chapter, their thoughts are created not through their understanding but by what is around them.

Many of our views of ourselves are determined by our surroundings early on. If our words carry such power, we must ensure they are always filled with the power to build up! As the apostle Paul stated, "And never let ugly or hateful words come from your mouth, but instead let your words become beautiful gifts that encourage others; do this by speaking words of grace to help them" (Ephesians 4:29 TPT).

Before proceeding, take some time and list some hateful or ugly words people have said to you, or you have said about yourself. Now, next to those words or statements, write the opposite. Then challenge yourself to only say what's on the right side of that sheet of paper! I promise you that you will feel better about yourself because there are new words you choose to believe to be true about who you are. You can, in turn, begin speaking words of positivity and affirmations for those around you and hopefully improve their self-perception too. Decide today, right now, that you will be the difference in whatever circle or tribe you are a part of.

Early in the book, I spoke about how the first brain is our subconscious, and it's in recording mode especially early in life. Every word spoken to us in our lives is recorded as truth. As we continue growing and our consciences come into action, we assemble everything that formulates our mindsets or perspectives. In effect, we become human echoes of all the words we allow to bounce around in our minds and spirits. Have you ever heard a strong echo in a cave? The sound is amplified and more repetitive than the original words shouted. When we allow harmful and toxic words to ruminate in our minds, our lives echo the vibration of all the negativity of those we meet.

Please note that in the developmental parts of our lives (in the first seven years, characterized by the delta and theta states), we have no say over our environment. While this seems unfair, during this time, our lives started shaping how we think about everything self and others, life and death, good and bad. What is astonishing is that we had no say-so. The essence of who we are is shaped by others' words, whether good or bad. It has so much to do with our surroundings, parents, media, culture, associates, and family. But if you're brought up in the right environment, usually you are on your way to a successful life! Our environment becomes "our" software! This is almost like when a computer is bought. While it can be powerful and effective, much depends on the software installed initially.

While this is not always the case, if our upbringing is the opposite (with child abuse, careless words, and a hostile atmosphere), we'll have more challenges than most. This is not a reason to blame our lack of success entirely on our environments, but our original settings were altered at the beginning of our lives. Thank God there is something we can do to fix it. We can shape our future as it should be by resetting, renewing, and returning to the original settings.

Science and neuroscience have verified these statements to be true and accurate. Words create who we are in the subconscious. Proverbs 22:6 NIV states, "Start children off on the way they should go, and even when they are old, they will not turn from it." This scripture shows Solomon's powerful statement about children and the truth. If we expose children to the knowledge of who they are and that they are unique and called for greatness, they become. This is a way of creating a generation without limits! If you have children and implement these settings into the hardwiring of their hearts, they are more likely to grow up and function without limits!

When I was younger, I was exposed to mayonnaise. Now, this wasn't any ordinary mayonnaise. This was Hellmann's mayonnaise—the most significant creation ever to land on a ham and cheese sandwich! (Well, other than the ham and cheese, that is.) One day after I had tasted Hellmann's mayonnaise on my sandwich, my mother tried to trick me and put some cheap knockoff mayonnaise on my sandwich, and I almost cried myself to death. I'm kidding. I knew immediately that it wasn't the original! What if we could get our children used to their original settings? What if they also were so used to the godly settings that they would spot a counterfeit setting and reject it? Only when the truth is understood can a lie be revealed.

The Bible says, "For as he thinks in his heart, so is he" (Proverbs 23:7 AMP). What are the words you have instilled in your heart? How often do you dwell on these words? Are they words that create a set way of thinking? Ultimately, the words we believe to be true about ourselves become who we are. Our perceptions are based on words, perhaps established long ago, that made us who we are.

The primary purpose of negative words is to reach your heart. Negative comments become the thief of the life and purpose God has called us to. Jesus said, "The thief comes only to steal, kill, and destroy" (John 10:10 NIV).

Words are like seeds and have DNA inside of them. Whether good or bad, words spoken to us quickly take root inside us. Once we allow them into our minds and give them attention, they flourish. This reminds me of the story I shared that occurred at the age of ten, spoken about in the previous chapter of the power of subconscious programming through words of when I played the game Monopoly. What was just a game became true because It reached my subconscious.

The principles outlined throughout this chapter have the power to transform - only if they are applied. The application of the principle of words can be summed up as follows:

- Words matter. Whether we realize it or not, words are woven into the fabric of our identities. These words became the foundations by which we now function positively and negatively.
- We must be careful and more cognizant of the words we allow to be spoken over our lives, for those words contain the seeds of what we are to become.
- We have the power to choose the seeds that grow within us. We now may determine whether the gardens of our thought lives will be full of grass or weeds.

Are you happy? Do you think there's more out there for you, or is this all you have? Do you feel like you have temporal peace or peace that surpasses all understanding, as Jesus stated in the book of Philippians? Is it possible that you can create a life that encompasses the peace that Jesus mentions? The Creator created creation to create. Are you creating, or are you in chaos? You can't be in both at the same time. Are you creating what you want in life? We were made in God's image. His word created all of creation. God loved the Word so much that he even called his son the Word. In the following chapters, we will dive deeper into the understanding and the power of words.

The Greek word used for "word" is "Logos." Britannica defines "Logos "as "the power that gives order, form, and meaning to the cosmos." When God, the Father, sent his son into the world, the apostle John, one of Jesus's closest disciples, called Jesus "the Word." Through John, God revealed to us that God entered the world and gave it order, form, and meaning through his word. Isn't it interesting that the things missing in the first creation ("the world was empty, without form and void" [Genesis

1:2 KJV]) were the very things that Jesus encompassed by being the logos (order, form, and meaning) of God? In this chapter, we will see how God's logos are meant to be our example as we allow our words to bring order, form, and meaning to our lives and those around us.

"In the beginning, God created the heavens and the earth … the earth was formless and empty, and darkness was over the surface of the deep" (Genesis 1:1–2 NIV). This is very important God spoke, and the unseen became seen through His Word. I want you to understand this because as "He is, so are we in this world" (1 John 4:17b NKJV). We're created like him, possessing the power of words to create.

This is one of the many reasons he delegated that responsibility to men in the garden when it was time to name the animals. Genesis 2:19–20 (NIV) reads, "Now the Lord God had formed out of the ground all the wild animals and all the birds in the sky. He brought them to the man to see what he would name them, and whatever the man called each living creature, that was its name. So, the man gave names to all the livestock, the birds in the sky, and all the wild animals." Whatever a person, place, or thing was named also indicated the nature that person, place, or thing was meant to manifest. When the man in the garden called it a lion, he released within the lion all the characteristics of that lion. In the same way, we will be learning that our words release the divine nature within us, which is filled with righteousness, peace, and joy, or the corrupt nature that comes from outside, which is filled with sin, fear, and doubt. We get to choose!

"Beloved, I pray that in all respects you may prosper and be in good health, just as your soul prospers" (3 John 1:2 NKJV). If your body and mind align, your soul and spirit prosper. I've invested so much in this subject that Matrix University was born from all this wisdom. The purpose is to return people to their original settings. The building blocks to restoration are through his words.

CHAPTER 5

WITCHES WARLOCKS & OCCULT

I'd like to take this chapter to dive deeper and discuss a topic that has captivated the minds of philosophers, scholars, and poets throughout the ages: the supernatural power of words. Words, as we know, possess an extraordinary ability to shape our thoughts, influence our actions, and ultimately define who we are as individuals and as a society. However, what many fail to recognize is that the power of words can stem from two distinct sources of origin– darkness, and light.

Let us first explore the supernatural power of words that emerge from the darkness. In the depths of human history, we have witnessed the destructive force of words used to spread hatred, incite, violence, and sow discord among communities. Words have been employed as weapons, tearing apart nations, marriages, relationships, and communities and fueling conflicts that have scarred our collective memory. The darkness that emanates from these words is a reminder of the immense responsibility we bear when we choose how to express ourselves.

But amidst this darkness, there is also a flash of hope. For it is through the supernatural power of words that we can shed light on the injustices that plague our world. Words can expose corruption, challenge oppressive systems, and ignite movements for change. Think of the great speeches that have rallied nations, the powerful poems that have given voice to the voiceless, and the courageous stories that have inspired generations. These words, born from the light, have the potential to illuminate the path toward a better future.

The supernatural Words of light have the remarkable ability to uplift, inspire, and heal. They can bring comfort to the broken-hearted, encouragement to the discouraged, and hope to the despairing. The light that radiates from these words has the power to transform lives, ignite passion, and foster unity among diverse individuals.

In a world often plagued by negativity, it is the power of positive words that can create a ripple effect of kindness and compassion. A simple act of speaking words of encouragement to someone who is struggling can have a profound impact on their journey. The light that emanates from these words has the potential to illuminate the darkest corners of our souls, reminding us of our shared humanity and the power we hold to make a difference.

So, as we navigate the vast landscape of understanding words, let us remember the duality of their power. We must be mindful of the darkness that can be unleashed through words of hatred and division, and let us strive to use our words to bring light into the world. Let us choose our words carefully, for they have the power to shape our reality, to build bridges instead of walls, and to inspire greatness within ourselves and others.

The power of words is a force that can either perpetuate darkness or illuminate the world with light. It is up to us, as individuals, to harness this power responsibly and consciously. We must choose words that heal, words that inspire, unite, that build, and that edify. In doing so, we can create a world where the power of words becomes a force for positive change, a force that brings us closer to the realization of a brighter, more compassionate future.

Let's dive into a story located in Matthew Chapter 12, in which Jesus starts denoting the two kingdoms and how both operate from spoken words. "Jesus knew their thoughts and replied, "Any kingdom divided by civil war is doomed. A town or family splintered by feuding will fall apart. And if Satan is casting out Satan, he is divided and fighting against himself. His own kingdom will not survive. And if I am empowered by Satan, what about your exorcists? They cast out demons, too, so they will condemn you for what you have said. But if I am casting out demons by the Spirit of God, then the Kingdom of God has arrived among you." (Matthew 12:25-28 NLT)

Jesus clearly states the presence of two supernatural kingdoms one of light and the other of darkness. He was speaking a word over the unclean spirits and they obeyed his word. Jesus started explaining kingdoms and the fact that they can not come against each other. That's division. If Satan drives out all of Satan, how will his kingdom (denoting there is an organized kingdom of darkness where all evil stems from) stand? He goes on to say there is a kingdom of light when he states that when the kingdom of light appears with its superiority, everything has to listen to Jesus' words, demonstrating the superior kingdom of God has arrived all through words that stem from the light. He said this because the Pharisees accused him of being the devil by casting out dark forces. Notice both kingdoms operate under words? The difference is the position of the heart. Jesus' heart is positioned with the father of light, while the kingdom of darkness is positioned with evil.

King Solomon stated in Proverbs that the tongue has the power of life and death. This chapter is called The Witches, Warlock, and the Occult, because only recently I realized one big factor of my 30-year journey in the spiritual world was that these powers that operate within evil are primarily accomplished by using words. We must understand that the kingdom of light leads to life, while the kingdom of darkness leads to death. Later in the book, I will give you scientific evidence of the power of words in their frequency and how there are high-frequency words and low-frequency words. They hold immense power and influence in our lives– words and their frequency. We must understand words are the building blocks of communication. They are the tools we use to express our thoughts, emotions, and ideas. And the position of our hearts when we use these words can shape our relationships, our perceptions, and even our own self-image. "Would you look for olives hanging on a fig tree or go to pick figs from a grapevine? Is it possible that fresh and bitter water can flow out of the same spring? So neither can a bitter spring produce fresh water." (James [Jacob] 3:11-12 TPT) So it is with the position of our hearts and the words that flow from the heart.

Witches and warlocks use their dark forces for spells, I'm quite aware of their power. They use words or spells but the position of their hearts is towards the dark side. They primarily use words to divide, to hurt, and to spread negativity. We can all become a witch or warlocks and destroy or be priests and build we get to choose. We live in a world where words are often thrown around carelessly, without considering the impact they may have on others. The position of our hearts, when we use derogatory language, insults, or hurtful remarks, can damage relationships, breed animosity, and create a toxic environment. Have you ever noticed how certain words, when repeated over and over, lose their meaning? They become background noise, losing their impact and significance. This phenomenon, known as semantic satiation, highlights the importance of using words thoughtfully and sparingly.

Moreover, the position of our hearts with which we use certain words can shape our own self-perception. If we constantly use negative words to describe ourselves, such as "stupid" or "worthless," we begin to internalize these beliefs. Conversely, we become witches or warlocks and create spells on ourselves. I'm sure you never thought you've done witchcraft but when we allow negative words to repeat themselves in our mind constantly we become someone who does spells on ourselves. If we use positive and empowering words from the kingdom of GOD and put on the garments of priests such as "capable" or "resilient," or with "God all things are possible" we start to see ourselves in a more positive light. The position of our heart with which we speak these words to ourselves can have a profound effect on our self-esteem and overall well-being. Words are not just mere sounds or symbols; they hold immense power. The position of our heart with which we use words can either create life or death.

In Matthew, Jesus makes a strong compelling statement "I will give you the keys of heaven's kingdom realm to forbid on earth that which is forbidden in heaven, and to release on earth that which is released in heaven." Matthew 16:19 TPT. That's a powerful statement! We have keys that represent power in our words. Keys represent authority, access, and privilege. I believe many times we don't understand the power we have. We knock on doors that we already have a key to use. But we use the key for the wrong things in our lives and can hold onto keys that we never use. We place curses on ourselves unknowingly. We place our words against us and we become our stumbling blocks. It's so easy to be driven into negativity. It's all around us. The influence is real. We capture what we see all around us, speak negative dialogue within ourselves, and then wonder why nothing positive happens in our lives.

I'm experienced in this world of darkness because, at the age of 25, I had someone tell me my future using tarot cards. At the moment, I didn't believe what I heard. I looked at it as a joke, only for the lady to tell me what was about to happen in my life years later, which happened! They had my attention, this led my life into the realm of bondage to darkness. My encounter bred a reality for me that lasted a segment of 10 years. I realized on my journey from darkness to light that, just like those who follow the light, darkness also uses words and spells to access a higher power.

Witches, warlocks, and the occult continue to be associated with mysterious supernatural powers, spells, and enchantments. While some may argue that these practices are harmless or even beneficial, it is crucial to acknowledge the negative aspects that can arise from delving into the world of witchcraft. In John 10:7-9 (NKJV) it states, "Then Jesus said to them again, "Most assuredly, I say to you, I am the door of the sheep. All who ever came before Me are thieves and robbers, but the sheep did not hear them. I am the door. If anyone enters by Me, he will be saved, and will go in and out and find pasture." Think of the spiritual realm with many doors. There are other ways of entering the spiritual realm Jesus states they are thieves that come to steal, kill, and destroy but Jesus states He is the way, He is the door no one goes to the Father except through Him.

Firstly, let us address the concept of spells. Spells are incantations or rituals performed to manipulate the natural order of things that I have witnessed firsthand. While some may argue that spells are merely a form of self-expression or a way to manifest desires, we must recognize the potential dangers they pose. Spells can be used to harm others, manipulate their thoughts, or even cause physical ailments. The power to control and manipulate others through spells is a grave violation of their autonomy and free will.

Furthermore, the practice of witchcraft often involves summoning and interacting with supernatural entities. I remember my visit to the Dominican Republic. The medium would ask me who I wanted to speak to. They were all identified with names and colors, for example, one entity was called Candelo his color was red. The medium would put a red bandana on, lay back, breathe in deeply, and the entity would possess her. I would be interacting for that session with Candelo hearing about future things to come. These entities, whether demons, spirits, or otherworldly beings, have evil intentions. By engaging with these entities, witches, and warlocks expose themselves to the risk of being influenced or possessed by dark forces. This can lead to losing control over one's actions and descending into darkness and chaos which I experienced for ten years.

The pursuit of witchcraft can lead to a dangerous obsession with power and control. The desire for power can consume individuals, blinding them to the consequences of their actions. I remember when I started my journey on the dark side it was all about external success. I started my car dealership with four cars and within seven years I had three car dealerships with over two hundred cars. Only then did I realize that true success is not material things but rather peace of heart. At this point in my life, I was externally rich but spiritually poor. This thirst for power can drive witches and warlocks to commit heinous acts, such as curses, hexes, or even human sacrifices. The negative consequences of such actions can ripple through families, marriages, relationships, and communities, causing fear, suffering, and destruction.

Moreover, the practice of witchcraft often involves secrecy and deception. Witches and warlocks may hide their true intentions and actions, leading to a lack of trust and transparency. This secrecy can breed fear and suspicion, creating community divisions and conflicts. The manipulation and exploitation of others for personal gain can erode the very fabric of trust that ideally holds societies together.

While the world of witches and warlocks may seem enchanting and alluring, it is essential to recognize the negative aspects of their practice. Spells, supernatural entities, the pursuit of power, and secrecy can all lead to harmful consequences for individuals and communities. These are all things that I encountered during my 10 years in the occult. We must approach these practices with caution and skepticism, ensuring that we do not fall prey to the dark side of witchcraft.

Occult

The Occult is a portal that we can open up, and we don't know it because we're often unaware. The occult means something that is hidden. And the enemy's biggest job is for you not to know that he's there, that's his biggest weapon in his arsenal. Ignorance is a place of darkness, and darkness is a place where Satan is the prince of darkness. His job is to keep us ignorant and allow him to maneuver his way through our lives. I remember my first visit to the Dominican Republic to visit the medium. She took me to the room that she considered to be the sacred room. There she had an altar set up. It was a ledge with many saints on it. In the middle of the room was a really small statue of Jesus. I asked the medium, why was Jesus smaller than all the other entities. She answered that they are all his helpers so they are bigger because they work for him as if somehow Jesus needs help. This my friend is called the occult; hiding the truth.

I'll give you a little rundown of how I have been able to understand the occult. Most pastors speak from a distant, biblical perspective. However, I can address the concept of the occult from a personal, biblical perspective since I have participated in it firsthand for ten years. I sat down with demons and spoke to them like it was an ordinary thing. It started during my youth because it seems like the occult, witchcraft, or spells are usually brought down from generation to generation. So, if your mom did it, odds are you're going to do it, and you're going to keep buying candles, and putting stuff on it, and it becomes an altar to the kingdom of darkness. It is something that is a portal into your life, and it usually grows.

When I was around ten or eleven years old, I went to my aunt's house and watched her perform witchcraft rituals. She had an assortment of different statutes with South Asian-like features. So, my mom went and started collecting statues to live in our home. And so, I was raised in these traditions. My journey started when I had my encounter with the occult at 25, I felt a connection since I was already pretty familiar with the lifestyle. When someone reads your cards, there's a spirit of divination, but it's opening a portal to a dark kingdom you will have to pay the price for in time. And you don't know how deep the occult can descend you into darkness. That's why it's called the occult, it is hidden.

Let's dive into the practice of the occult, especially for evil purposes. When we think of witchcraft, witches, and warlords, we often think of spells. They often go into this big book and put all these spells together. The primary building block of spells is words, so once again, we see the importance of words in determining whether we are interacting with the kingdom of light or the kingdom of darkness.

Popular culture uses new-age practices to put a value on rocks, chanting, and sage just to name a few. There is a search for the spiritual world but after reflecting further, we should consider who is the source behind these practices. These things may seem good, but they must come from God, the creator of the world. Remember Jesus stated he is the door any other way they are thieves.

To spell is to write or name the letters that form words in sequence. So, that's what spelling is, right? Anything in a sentence that's a sequence. A spoken word or formal word held to magic power, a state of enchantment, a strong compelling influence or attraction. So, spells can be anything that you speak or someone speaks over you.

In my routine visit to the Dominican Republic, to meet my medium, she would ask, "What do you want?" And she would speak it out over a candle so both kingdoms of light and darkness understood this. Both kingdoms operate primarily on words. Jesus said ask and it shall be given, and so, if both kingdoms operate in the same realm of words, then we should be mindful of the words we are hearing and using.

The power of words is mighty. When God empowers us, he empowers the words we speak. So, we have to be careful about our inner speech because whatever it is that is going on within us, it's already what's going on inside of our hearts. If you have established a word or statement, such as "I'm never going to be successful," then you've theoretically become a witch or warlock because that statement (spell) becomes an altar, and that altar becomes the occult to hide from the truth that God placed inside of you. And so we can create altars by our spellings. If we're not careful in what we accept as our identity, we will have an altered identity of truth. I want you to understand what God says, not the opinion you have of yourself or what someone has given to you. Because the minute you are fixed on one opinion, that becomes your altar.

Repentance is a change of mind. It is exchanging a truth for a lie. For the first 28 years of our lives, we're conditioned mostly negatively around our circumstances and environment, and nobody checks to see what we allow to be true. We started building identities in lies that were not true. The only way that anything's going to shift in your life is by acknowledging what truth is and making sure it reaches your heart and replaces whatever lies the enemy has used.

Look at what Solomon says to further help you understand that every word you speak has weight. Proverbs 18:21 (NKJV) states, "The tongue has the power of life and death, and those who love it will eat its fruit." We have the power of life and death within our lips. But what I want to zoom in on is your inner speech. Our words have the power to create in us the ability to be warlocks and witches or to be priests. We're the ones who create these altars. And well, how do we create altars? Okay, we know that spells are words put together. Words put together have power. And when there's negative self-talk inside of us, then those negative conversations become our altars. Because we believe the lies and where our belief goes so does our faith.

So, Satan doesn't have to do anything besides whisper negativity into us, and we believe it and create internal altars. And though we're trying to get closer to God, we're creating the occult within ourselves, hiding what God has in us. We know this negativity is not from God because God is saying, "You're perfect." God says, you're whole, you're beautiful, you're the apple of his eye, right? But we create these altars that are opposite. We create altered identities upon these altars. So, it's the opposite of what God is saying. We want God to move in us, but we don't realize the altars we already have built within ourselves that don't serve him.

We don't realize what vows we've made of darkness. I made a vow after my first failed marriage and said to myself, "I will never again marry." I had become a warlock and created an altar where I worshiped because it was my truth. I made a vow that I would never leave my heart open to a woman. And God himself had to help me destroy it. The altar I had created had to be broken for me to welcome love again into my life. If we complete an internal inventory of how many vows, conscious or unconscious, we have made or how many altars we have established without realizing the consequences perhaps in this we will find our change.

Our inner conversations are a good place to understand what we believe to be true about ourselves. It's a good place to go and say, "Hold on, there is something I've created, some kind of vow that I've built an altar for. Is this helping or hurting me? Does this align with what God says about me?" We must be aware of our inner speech and the altars we have created unknowingly because we are trying to access God while still wearing witches and warlock garments instead of priestly garments. This inner conflict will continue until we are aware and destroy altars that are altering our lives from their original settings. I hope this has opened up your eyes to the understanding of the power of words and their origins. Awareness is the first step to change. Later in the book, you will be given tools to put into practice that can help you get this done.

CHAPTER 6

PROOF IS IN THE PUDDING

Preaching the gospel of grace for many years, I realized something was missing. After people were saved, they would still battle hurt, soul wounds, and mental strongholds. I prayed and fasted and was inevitably led to Alaska, where my exploration of inner healing began. This journey awoke within me a desire to show all those I encountered to start an emotional intelligence journey that would ultimately empower them to overcome mental obstacles as they reigned in life. This journey led me to Dr. Caroline Leaf, Joseph Dispenza, Bruce Lipton, and, most recently, Dr. Masaru Emoto.

Dr. Masaru Emoto wrote "The Hidden Meanings in Water," and his findings have revolutionized my way of looking at words. According to Genesis, the most momentous event in the universe is when God spoke words that made the unseen visible. This is a tremendous power.

Before I continue this chapter, I want to acknowledge that other scientists have criticized Dr. Emoto's findings in his book, "The Hidden Meanings in Water." As with many scientific experiments, there is often pushback related to how specific processes were carried out or how findings are recorded. However, I am choosing to exercise faith and believe in the possibility that many truths are embedded in Dr. Emoto's research and experimental findings. His work aligns with spiritual truths. It also acts as another witness to validating God's word. So, for the remainder of this chapter, I will speak from the standpoint of belief in Dr. Emoto's experiment on water and the power of words.

The element called water has a close relation to words. Dr. Emoto found that water can record words. Words carry frequencies, according to the beliefs of Dr. Emoto. He was able to freeze water so that he could see the effects of words on the water in its frozen state, and his findings supported the notion that words can indeed affect water.

"The average human body contains 70% water. We start our life 99% water as fetuses. When we are born, we are 90% water, and by the time we reach adulthood, we are down to 70%. If we die of old age, we will probably be about 50% water; in other words, we exist mostly as water throughout our lives. From a physical perspective, humans are water. When we realize this, we can see life differently and acknowledge the water's effects on our lives" (Dr. Masaru Emoto, The Hidden Meanings in Water).

We see in Genesis how God's very breath hovered over the water (Genesis 1:2 NIV). Then we see how one water sphere was called heaven while another was called earth, which became the foundation of all life. We can read how, over and over, wells were places where God would meet his people. Even in one of the most famous conversations of Jesus we have documented, he is sitting next to a well and telling a Samaritan woman, "If you knew the gift of God and who you are speaking to, you would ask me, and I would give you living water" (John 4:10 NIV). We see clearly that the water is symbolic of life, and it must be flowing. Notice that the waters spoken about in the word are rivers, not still water. From this point of view, I can see how people should live their lives. And how do we do it? We can start by purifying the body, which is 70 percent water, to eliminate the toxins that have taken us away from our original settings of health.

The water and blood in the bodies of sick people are usually stagnant. When blood stops flowing, the body starts to decay. If the blood in your brain stops flowing, it can be life-threatening. But why does the blood become stagnant? We can see this condition as the stagnation of emotions. Modern researchers have shown that the mind's condition directly impacts the body's condition. Living a full and enjoyable life makes you feel better physically, mentally, and spiritually. On the other hand, when your life is filled with struggles, sorrow, and pain, your body knows it. It is one of the ways the body talks to you to say something is wrong. I call it the "check engine light." The body is flashing to you, saying, "Help." So, when your positive emotions flow throughout your body, you feel a sense of joy as you transition towards physical health, moving, changing, and flowing. This is what life is all about.

According to John 10:10 (NIV), Jesus came to give us life and the ability to live more abundantly. This is the greatest moment in time when science is validating God's truth even though they will never fully affirm it as such because science and faith are like oil and vinegar, we have ears to hear and know that God is using the scientific community to discover what we have heard for many years. God is allowing the word to be revealed and experienced with the hope that we will dive into the waters of this abundance in some way, shape, or form.

Dr. Emoto stated he "studied water for many years [and] the realization that water can copy information has changed his life. After making this discovery in America, he brought it back to Japan and has since used the information copying function of water to help people recover their health." This is a profound finding. There hasn't been a more significant time than now because science corroborates what God has been saying for hundreds of years. Science can directly verify the power of words. In Dr. Emoto's experiment, he was able to capture the frequencies of words and see the variations of these frequencies, allowing the world to see the invisible becoming visible.

When your heart is open to possibilities, you notice small things that can lead to enormous discoveries. Dr. Emoto states that he learned that no two snowflakes are the same. All are different designs, though similar. If snowflakes are made from the same water, how can they freeze differently? What makes the difference in snowflakes?

So, he started his experiment with water. After two months, he finally got one photograph of beautiful hexagonal crystals. Emoto was filled with excitement. I am in awe of how snowflakes started Dr. Emoto's quest for findings that could revolutionize how we see ourselves, our thoughts, and our emotions. As humans, we are 70 % water. And if I am 70 % water, what messages am I carrying? What am I reflecting on the world? As you continue reading, you will see how this connects with the facts relating to the power of words spoken out loud and the inner speech we have within ourselves. We don't need faith to believe this truth about what we're saying concerning the power of words because science is coming alongside and cosigning these truths; whether we believe it or not, truth is truth. So, let's dig into Dr. Emoto's findings in his experiment.

Water Is the Mirror of the Soul

"Water is a mirror to the soul that has many faces forming and aligning itself with the conscience of humans. What gives water the ability to reflect what is hidden in the soul?

First, I want to ensure that you understand that existence is vibration. The universe is in a constant state of vibration, where each thing generates its own frequency you will find that it has a unique vibration. The science of quantum mechanics generally acknowledges that a substance is just a vibration. When we separate something into the smallest part of the smallest part, we enter a strange world where all that exists is particles and waves. The invisible sustains the particles. According to civil engineer Trevor English, "Every human on planet Earth is made up of millions and millions of atoms, which all are 99% empty space." Just this understanding brings us into another realm of comprehension of how much space we have versus particles.

One of his findings relates to tap water from Tokyo. When he tried to freeze it to see what it looked like, he saw nothing because it included chlorine used to sanitize it. Therefore, because it had been tampered with, it created nothing. An important takeaway from this finding is that anything contaminated cannot be formed into anything beautiful. Think about this notion applied to us if our thoughts are contaminated by negative thinking, this influences 70 % of who we are (water). This is similar to when God was looking over the water and saw darkness and no form—chaos. However, within natural water, no matter where—in natural springs, underground rivers, glaciers, and river's upper reaches— Emotto found complete crystals were born. This was one of Dr. Emoto's many experiments regarding the crystallization of contaminated versus pure water.

The Music Within

As you surely know, music is made of vibrations, sometimes including words. In one of Dr. Emoto's experiments, he put a bottle of water on a table and put two speakers alongside it, exposing the water to music. The water was distilled so that he could clearly see the water crystals. The first music he used was Beethoven's Pastoral Symphony. The results were fully formed crystals. He moved on to Mozart's Symphony No. 8, a grateful prayer to beauty; that also formed elegant crystals. He then used Chopin's étude in E, Op. 10, which also surprised him with stunning results. Water was exposed to classical music which created beautiful, elegant, and exciting crystals with distinctive characteristics. So, of course, he wanted to find out what would happen with the opposite type of music. When he did this experiment with heavy metal music, the results were fragmented and malformed crystals. I am not trying to condemn heavy metal, but Dr. Emoto's findings demonstrate that even the music we listen to directly impacts how we carry our lives. What is being memorized in the water within us? This is an interesting question.

Could this be a significant factor in how we carry ourselves and our well-being, what we reflect to the world, and the vibrations people sense when we arrive somewhere? When I started reading this, it just made me more aware that I am responsible for everything I expose myself to and that I have a responsibility to my future by making decisions to allow in my life everything that is only going to add to my life, not take away from it. I'm sure that if you're reading this, some self-reflection is going on, and you are evaluating and even realizing that what you hear has an effect. But the research didn't stop there; that was only the beginning.

Writings on the Wall

In another experiment, Dr. Emoto wanted to go further with the findings, so he asked himself, "What would happen if we labeled the bottles with words?" In other words, he would write positive and negative words and flip them around labeling the water. He used words like "thank you" and "fool." It didn't seem logical for water to be able to "read" the writings, understand the meaning, and change form. We understand that the intention and position of the heart before writing it caused a different effect.

Dr. Emoto said he felt like he and his team were explorers on a journey through an untouched jungle. The results of this experiment would shock the scientific community. The water exposed to "thank you" formed the beautiful hexagonal crystals. At the same time, the word "fool" produced crystals similar to the water exposed to heavy metal music, with the crystals malformed and fragmented.

Please stop for a second and realize the implications of this. Consider how many labels have been put on us and led us to become those labels even though they're not based on truth because whatever we accept as truth becomes our truth even though it is not valid. Labels are so powerful. With this study, we can deepen our understanding of the implications of labels that we accept as truth, being that we now know that since we are 70% water, these labels are placing a message within us that is resounding throughout our bodies and causing the wrong creative nature to be activated in us.

When we memorize the Word of God, we become the Word. These are the labels that we should put on ourselves. When we study scripture, we're learning it not only in our minds and hearts but also in our beings because we are 70% water, and whatever resounding conversation we have within us is being memorized by our bodies and ultimately determining who we become.

Please take a minute to dissect these findings, and as you think about this, realize how many labels you have been carrying around. Now science is saying it's in your being! It's part of who you are because you accept it as truth. The lesson that we can learn from this experiment has to do with the power of words. The vibrations of good words positively affect our world and us, whereas the vibrations from negative words can destroy us and those around us. Learning about water is like exploring how the cosmos works or like a portal into another dimension. I will continue digging into this phenomenon of truth found by science only to corroborate what God has been saying for thousands of years—that the mouth has the power of life and death.

Emoto speaks about a particular bottle he labeled with "love and gratitude." It was as if the water rejoiced and celebrated by creating a picture of a flower in bloom; it was so beautiful that it changed his life! From that moment on, water has taught me the delicacy of the human soul and the impact love and gratitude can have on the world. In Japan, the words of the soul are said to reside in the spirit called Gato Dama, or the spirit of the word. The act of speaking words has the power to change the world. Words enormously influence how we think and feel, and things generally go more smoothly when positive words are used. However, up until now, we have never been able to physically see the effects of positive words as we have with Dr. Emoto's experiment.

Imagine if everything we have in our minds and hearts is the love of God, and it's demonstrated through our gratitude as a reciprocal response to the love of God. Can you imagine your entire being immersed in the Father's love, which resonates within us and is found in our minds, bodies, and souls? If we received every message resembling the love of God, what would our love lives look like? How would those around us be affected? Could it be that understanding the way we carry love can bring us deeper into the knowledge of the Father's love? Could it be that we are the light within the darkness that others can feel every morning when we approach them? The deep love we receive every morning becomes the well of humanity. I want to challenge you to think about these findings and how they can affect our lives. It has affected me; I'm sure it will affect you too. Later, I will teach practical ways to do this, but for now, let's get an even deeper understanding.

In Dr. Emoto's faith-meets-science journey, the following studies were conducted and documented in his book The Hidden Messages in Water. He was able to show the effects words and labels have on water.

Love and gratitude/You make me sick

In his research, they wrote words on a piece of paper and wrapped the paper around the bottle of water. On one bottle they wrote love and gratitude, and to their astonishment, perfect crystals were formed, indicating that love and gratitude are fundamental to the phenomenon of life in all nature.

There was another bottle in which they wrote the words "You make me sick" and "I will kill you." When these words which indicate harm to humans were shown to the water it created deformed crystals. It even appeared that the words you make me sick created the shape of a man holding a gun. This was after they crystallized the water that was labeled.

Angel/Satan

As the studies continued, there was another bottle that was labeled Angel, and the other bottle was labeled Satan. The results again were too powerful to ignore. The word angel resulted in a ring of small crystals linked together. They look like a bunch of little diamonds, and they were glued together to make a perfect circle, while the word Satan forms a crystal with a dark lump in the center, sort of like looking at a black hole when you look into heaven, it was formless and without life.

You're cute/you fool

Dr. Emoto then conducted a test at an elementary school. After the children said "You're cute" over the water. The water was then crystallized and the results were astonishing. They became perfect snowflakes with diamonds inside similar to all the other findings but the water spoken over with you fool looked like small, deserted islands without life. These findings are extraordinary for us to understand without a reasonable doubt that our words carry frequencies and depending on the position of your heart words can distort something or they can create something. Now we're not asking for your faith because these tests have proven that low-frequency words can never create anything beautiful.

In another fascinating scientific experiment conducted by Dr. Emoto to investigate the potential influence of prayer on the physical properties of water, researchers set out to examine the effects of spoken words of affirmation over a lake. To ascertain any discernible changes, samples of the lake water were collected prior to and after the involvement of a priest who performed a prayer. The results of this experiment were truly astonishing. A noticeable transformation occurred within the time frame between the initial water sample and the sample taken after the prayer. It appeared that the vibrations generated by the priest's prayer had reached and affected the entire lake, resulting in a significant alteration in the information or "messages" contained within the water.

The precise mechanism through which the vibrations from the prayer influenced the water's composition and properties remains the subject of ongoing scientific inquiry. While the exact explanation may still elude us, it is important to note that numerous studies have previously demonstrated the potential impact of external factors, such as sound vibrations, on the physical properties of water. One possible explanation could be rooted in the concept of resonance, where the vibrational frequency of the spoken words of affirmation resonates with the molecular structure of the water, leading to a change in its inherent properties.

I will conclude by sharing Dr. Emoto's popular experiment involves three glass bowls filled with water and rice. It is called the rice experiment. Over a span of 30 days, he spoke different words to each bowl in order to examine the potential effects of language and intention on their contents.

In the first bowl, Dr. Emoto uttered the words "thank you" consistently. Surprisingly, after the 30-day period, the water and rice in this bowl began to undergo a process of fermentation. This unexpected result left Dr. Emoto astounded, suggesting that gratitude and positive language may have a transformative impact on the molecular structure of water and its surroundings.

Conversely, in the second bowl, Dr. Emoto repeatedly uttered the words "you idiot." To his surprise, the water and rice in this bowl turned black over time. This outcome indicated a negative influence of derogatory language and its potential to cause detrimental effects on the environment.

Curiously, in the third bowl, Dr. Emoto chose to completely ignore it, not speaking any specific words or directing any particular intention toward it. Astonishingly, the water and rice in this bowl also turned black, suggesting that neglect or indifference may have similarly negative consequences.

These findings shed light on the profound impact our words and intentions can have on our surroundings. Dr. Emoto's experiment serves as a reminder that the language we use and the energy we emit through our words can significantly influence our environment, both positively and negatively.

In a world where communication plays a vital role, it is crucial to be mindful of our choice of words. This experiment encourages us to consider the potential consequences of our language and serves as a reminder to cultivate a positive and respectful approach in our interactions. By doing so, we can contribute to a harmonious and healthy environment for ourselves and those around us.

Returning to the book of Proverbs, we have the power of life and death in what we say. The power of our prayer is proven over and over to be true; this makes my joy complete. I always believed what the Bible said and relied solely on faith to trust in God's promises. But we are in a time when faith is not needed as much to validate what God has been saying because, as I mentioned before, science is cosigning many aspects of God's word. Psalms 8:26 references that we are small gods, able to create from the invisible, just like the Father. Whether good or bad, we're constantly creating, but with this wisdom, we can be more intentional in our words because they contain the power to create.

CHAPTER 7

INNER CONVERSATION CREATE REALITY

Now that we've learned the effects of our use of words and our thoughts let's continue with discussing our inner conversation. Talking to oneself is a habit everyone indulges in. We could no longer stop talking to ourselves than we could stop eating and drinking. All we can do is control the direction of our inner conversation.

Most of us are unaware of this little piece of wisdom. Our internal conversations are often the cause of the circumstances in our lives. Think about this for a second.

We are told, "For as he thinks in his heart, so is he." (Proverbs 23:7 NKJV), but do we know that a person's thinking follows their inner conversation? In the direction in which they want to go, they must put off the former conversation (which is called in the Bible "the Old Man" and "the old stinking thinking") and be renewed in the spirit of their mind. Speech is the image of the mind. Words are powerful—so powerful that they pave the way and lead us to the future. What are we laying down?

Growing up, I remember going on the PATH train and always going to the front car because I wanted to see what was before me. A train will always reach a fork in the track and will travel according to the direction of the engineer. So, it is with us. Once we decide where to go with our internal dialog, the body, like a train, follows. This is profound. Therefore, to change our speech, we must first change our minds.

The world is a magic circle of infinite possible mental transformations or an infinite number of possible mental conversations. By "speech," I mean those mental chats we carry within ourselves. When people discover the creative power of inner talking, they will realize their function and mission in life. Early on in my journey of finding self, I learned this to be a significant truth. Only after this discovery can we act according to a purpose. Without such knowledge, we behave unconsciously, but as civilized beings, we must be aware of our inner chatter. Everything is a manifestation of the mental conversations that go on in us without our awareness.

Have you ever had a conversation with yourself and found yourself getting angry? - And you were only conversing with yourself. Think about it. Our inner-chat can be constructive or destructive. However, we must be aware that those internal conversations are the passageway that ultimately creates our destinies. This is a powerful truth. A person's inner dialogue attracts a future that will change his world for the better or worse. Living without changing our internal conversation is a struggle of many things. We can go around and around in the same toils and disappointment, blaming others, when indeed, we must blame our inner conversations because this leads us to purpose and destiny.

As civilized beings, we must become aware of our inner conversations and act purposefully. As long as there is no change in a person's inner talking, the person's destiny remains the same. Your familiar past will be your predictable future. The attempt to change the world before we change our inner dialogue is a struggle against the very nature of things. People can circle around in the same disappointments and misfortunes, not seeing them as caused by their negative inner talking but as caused by others. This may seem far-fetched, but it is a matter that lends itself to research and experimentation. Not until we change how we look at things will we see those matters differently; the change always starts in our inner conversations.

Our inner conversations represent the world we live in, in various ways—in our subjective worlds and our self-revelations of our inner speech. We abandon ourselves to negative inner talking, yet we expect to retain command of life. Our present mental conversations do not recede into the past, as people once believed. They advance into the future to confront us as wasted or invested words. "So shall my word be that goes forth from My mouth; It shall not return to Me void, but it shall accomplish what I please, And it shall prosper in the thing for which I sent it." (Isaiah 55:11 NKJV).

In today's society, we often fail to recognize the impact our attitudes have on others. Our fixed perspectives, influenced by preconceived notions and biases, hinder the kindness and generosity that could otherwise flourish within us. It is imperative that we take control of our inner dialogue and practice the art of shaping our thoughts.

By consciously directing our mental conversations, we tap into the immense power of our imagination. This canvas, bestowed upon us by God, allows us to transform and create, unleashing our creative energies from the realms of the mind and emotions to the physical world. The possibilities seem boundless, as the gift bestowed upon us by the divine holds no known limits. In embracing this ability, we unlock the thrill of becoming architects of our own reality. We become aware of the immense potential that lies within us to shape our interactions, relationships, and ultimately, our lives. By cultivating a professional tone in our inner dialogue, we foster a sense of empathy, understanding, and respect for others.

What is your aim? Does your inner talk match it? This conscious exercise makes every state of a person's progress of the imagination, the canvas of the mind, matching their inner speech to their fulfilled desire. What does this look like? As we control our inner talking, matching it to our fulfilled desires, we can lay aside all other processes. Then we act with clear imagination and intention. We've imagined the vision fulfilled and continue the mental conversations from that premise. The right inner speech is the speech that will be yours, and you will realize your ideal. In other words, it is the speech of fulfilled desire.

To assume a new concept of yourself is to change your inner conversation. It is, therefore, also referred to in scripture as putting on a new way of thinking. Though unheard by others, our inner conversation is more productive of future conditions than all the audible promises or threats of people. Your ideal is waiting to become a reality.

There are two gifts that God has bestowed upon humans alone and no other mortal creature. These two gifts are mind and speech, and the gifts of mind and speech are equivalent to the gift of eternal life. If people use these two gifts correctly, they will be brought into the truth. With the gift of mind and speech, you create the conditions and circumstances of life. "In the beginning was the Word, and the Word was with God, and the Word was God" (John 1:1 NIV).

You and your inner conversations, or words, are one. This flash of the most profound insight taught Paul to write. Put off your former self and way of thinking, which was corrupt, and renew your mind with God's spirit and word. To put on the new man and be renewed in the spirit of your mind is to change your inner conversation or speech and mind. A change in dialog is a change of mind.

The prophet Samuel said, "The Spirit of the LORD speaks by me; his word is on my tongue" (2 Samuel 23:2 NIV). If the Lord's Word was in the prophet's tongue, then the Lord's mouth that uttered the Word must be the prophet's mind, for inner conversations originate in the mind and produce tiny movements in the tongue. The prophet is telling us that the mouth of God is the mind of humanity and that our inner conversations should align with the Word of God. We are creating life about us as we create within ourselves.

In the Bible, we are told that "the word is very near to you; it is in your mouth and your heart, that you can do it. See, I have set before you today life and death good and evil" (Deuteronomy 30:14–15 ESV). The conditions and circumstances of life are not created by some power external to yourself. They are the conditions that result from exercising your freedom of choice—your freedom to choose the ideas to which you will respond.

If you want to reap success, you must plan success. The idea in your mind that starts the whole process is the idea you accept as true. The mind always behaves according to the assumption with which it starts. Therefore, to experience success, we must assume that we are successful. We must live on the level of the imagination itself, and it must be consciously and deliberately undertaken. It does not matter if, at the present moment, external facts deny the truth of your assumption. This is where faith comes in. Faith is being sure of the unseen. If you persist in your belief, it will become a fact.

In the later chapters, I will explore what specific scriptures you want to download as fundamental keys for changing your inner conversations. You must define the person you envision to be and then assume your vision is fulfilled. In faith, that assumption will find expression through you. The actual test of a religion is in its use, but men have made it a thing to defend. It is to you that the words are spoken. Blessed are those who believe, for they shall see and accomplish those things spoken to them by the Lord. Just try to conceive of yourself as the one you want to be and remain faithful to that. Try it and see whether life will not be more likely to shape itself on the model of your imagination, the canvas of the mind. Everything bears witness to the use or misuse of humanity's inner conversation. "Write down the revelation and make it plain on tablets so that a herald may run with it." (Habakkuk 2:2 NIV). Negative inner talk, particularly evil and envious chatter, is the breeding ground of future battlefields. People have developed a secret affection for these negative internal conversations through habit. Through them, they justify failure, criticize their neighbors, gloat over the distress of others, and, in general, pour out their venom on all.

Such misuse of the word perpetuates the violence of the world. The transformation of self requires that we meditate on a given frame—a phrase that implies our ideal is realized—and inwardly affirm it repeatedly until we are inwardly affected by its implication. Hold fast to your noble inner convictions or conversations. Nothing can take them from you but yourself. Nothing can stop them from becoming objective facts. All things generated out of your imagination by the Word of God produce life, which is your inner conversation. Therefore, every vision and dream reaps its own words, which were inwardly spoken.

The great secret of success is controlled in a conversation from a place of fulfilled desire. The only price you pay for success is giving up your former internal talk, which belongs to the old way of thinking. The time is ripe for many of us to take conscious charge of creating our destinies.

Consciously and voluntarily using our imaginations, the canvases of our minds, to inwardly hear and say only what is in harmony with our ideals is actively bringing heaven to earth. Whenever we exercise our imagination through inner talk, we design our future. Think of your internal chat as the paintbrush you use to prime the canvas of your future. Always use your imagination masterfully as a participant, not as an onlooker. Using our imagination, we transform energy from the mental–emotional level to the physical level to extend our senses. Imagine seeing what you want to see, hearing what you want to hear, and touching what you want to feel. Become intensely aware of doing so. Give your imaginary state all the tones and feelings of reality. Keep doing so until you arouse the mood of accomplishment and a sense of relief within yourself.

People refer to the imagination as a plaything or "the green screen." However, it is the very gateway to reality. Imagination is the way to the desired state. What you do in your imagination through inner conversation is the only important thing within the circle of your thinking.

Imagination is divine vision—the canvas of our minds. Imagination is life's preview of coming attractions. You are the director. Let's say I say the word giraffe right now in your imagination pops up a giraffe. All that we need is our words made visible. What we do not comprehend now is related by affinity to the unseen forces of our inner conversations and the moods they arouse within us. If we do not like what is happening to us, it is a sure sign that we need a change in our mental diet. "Jesus answered, 'It is written 'Man shall not live on bread alone, but on every word that comes from the mouth of God.'" (Matthew 4:4 NIV). Having discovered the mouth of God to be the minds of people, we should feed our minds only loving, noble thoughts, words, or fruitful inner conversations. That's how we build our world. Let God's lovely hands raise your hunger and thirst to all that is noble and has a good rapport.

CHAPTER 8

THE LOOKOUT

What's on your mind? People ask us this question in moments of silence while driving down the highway. Typically, we reply with one-word answers. "Nothing." even though it is usually not nothing. We have a lot on our minds. We spend more time in the unseen spiritual world of thought than speaking. If you are like me, you have too many thoughts. We may be thinking of a project we need to complete, a sermon that needs to be drawn up, a billboard we can't stand, or we're a little hungry because we saw an Applebee sign a mile back. Yet still, we answer, "Nothing."

We usually don't think of anything important when asked this question. We were letting our thoughts wander, and someone caught us doing it. Somehow, responding with, "I want a cheeseburger because I had the McDonald's jingle on loop in my head," doesn't seem remarkable. Imagine having to voice every thought that ran across our minds. Just the thought of it makes my stomach tighten.

Most people, including me, are usually unaware of what they are thinking about. At the same time, you know the impact that your thoughts can have on you. You can, for example, become depressed, angry, frustrated, lonely, disappointed, fearful, worried, sad, and doubtful. On the positive side, some thoughts can make you smile, laugh out loud, feel a sense of pride, relax, feel confident, or—when passing by a McDonald's—make you crave an ice-cold Coke.

Most of the time, your thoughts directly control how you feel at any given moment, regardless of whether you are consciously aware of it. With that in mind, wouldn't it be great if you could better control what you were thinking so that you could change how you are feeling at any time? Don't you want the wheel back? You can take it! As Caroline Leaf said, "We are thinking, feeling, and choosing all the time."

This chapter will put all the previous chapters into perspective. We must reset our original settings in our lives because our original settings have been altered. At my church, we have a soundboard. Its original settings worked for what we needed, but unfortunately, someone changed them, causing it to sound horrible! We knew automatically that someone had changed the original settings and caused a deviation in its function. The enemy of this world, even our ego, which is driven by past traumas wants to control, mute, press buttons, or even alter how you speak. That is because when something is altered, it's no longer suitable or able to function according to its design or purpose.

When we consider the anatomy of a smartphone, it becomes apparent that our minds too have the capacity to be altered from their original settings. Just as changing the settings on a phone can lead to malfunction, altering our mental state can result in a lack of proper functioning. It is important to recognize this and take the necessary steps to reset our minds, just as we would with a phone. By making an intentional hard reset, we can restore our minds one day at a time to their original settings and optimize their performance.

When our original settings have been altered, we are shifted to land elsewhere rather than the destination God has planned for us. One atomic-level change in a plane will shift and transform where the plane lands. One slight shift will make the aircraft miss its mark. So, it is with us; one traumatic experience, hurt, or pain in early childhood diverts us from what God originally intended. The enemy uses people, culture, family, and friends. They can be used to manipulate and shift our way of being, thinking, and seeing. In this chapter, I will bring light to our thought management so that our lives sound good and look good and our future is promising.

In the beginning, God created, and after completing something great, he looked and saw that it was good! That's how he looked at us when he created us in the womb. When we were woven together in the womb, he looked and said, "This is very good!"

For me, good has always been an exaggerated version of God. If you take out "o" the word "good," it spells "god." So, when God says something is good, it is an extended version of who he is. When he said we were excellent, I believe he was saying his creation was perfect! This is just one more way to emphasize how good God is. But something went wrong along the way after we were born, and that's what we must explore to reset back to our original settings. We must return to our original settings of awe and adoration—an environment allowing God's goodness to reign in every area of our lives.

We are explorers by nature. Exploration has captivated many men and women and drawn them toward what makes us God-like. This we can perceive from stories of great explorers like Apollo 11's Neil Armstrong. The mission was to land two men on the moon and safely bring them back to Earth. On July 16, 1969, the astronauts Neil Armstrong, Edwin "Buzz" Aldrin, and Michael Collins blasted off into the sky. We know humanity has dared to believe in the impossible and achieve it. Reaching the moon was impossible until those three astronauts did it.

We also know women who were pushing boundaries. Amelia Mary Earhart, born July 24, 1897, disappeared on July 2, 1937. She was an American aviation pioneer and author. Earhart was the first female aviator to fly solo across the Atlantic Ocean. What Armstrong and Earhart had in common was that they wanted to create spaces for the impossible by going with what they felt and saw in their minds and the eyes of their hearts.

"Then the LORD answered me and said, 'Write the vision and engrave it plainly on [clay] tablets so that the one who reads it will run'" (Habakkuk 2:2 AMP). I'm sure these great pioneers had imagined their successes before they materialized. People saw themselves on the moon before assembling even one piece of the shuttle. Before they explored the impossible they first explored their hearts to see it. Visions only arise from a deep exploration of your inner world. Many fail to explore the self where all the treasures are hidden. These pioneers were inner explorers before they ever became outer explorers.

Amelia saw herself flying away before she flew. Way before she even stepped onto a plane, she could draw the experience of flying from her creative nature. There she could feel the experience of flying, which she eventually could manifest in the physical world. These people are remembered for being fearless! Being fearless doesn't mean you won't be afraid; it means you overcame fear.

Nobody remembers fearful people because fear has little to do with the explorative and creative nature of all of us. The past experiences and failures of those mentioned above didn't cripple them; they could look beyond their failures and face fear head-on. Their pasts weren't perfect, but they didn't falter based on past hurts and disappointments. Instead, they saw success in their hearts. For most of us, that's not the case.

We view everything through the lenses of past failures such as "you will never achieve anything great." Perhaps this is what your father said to you when you were young; now it has become you. But that is not God's big idea for your life, and constantly viewing your life through past failures prevents you from living your best life. The echoes of the past stop us from entering the other side of fear, where the possibilities lie. These self-defeating, mismanaged thought patterns will not allow our creative nature to take off. Fear freezes our explorative nature and with insight into the problem we can counterattack fear with faith.

Emotional Intelligence (EQ)

What is Emotional Intelligence? Let's first understand that EQ is your ability to identify what you are feeling. In this invisible realm, it is important to be aware at all times, to discern a particular feeling, and how your feelings affect you and those around you. EQ represents our ability to control ourselves and our emotions through awareness of ourselves and others. Most Fortune 500 companies have an IQ (which is a number that measures someone's intelligence) and EQ test for higher-up positions that entail team building and management positions. Companies lean more toward recruiting candidates with high EQs than those with high IQs because those with higher EQs can read others and build teams more efficiently than the ones with higher IQs. The ability to self-manage emotions is highly sought after and the final frontier for us in leadership as EQ accounts for 90% of a Fortune 500 company's success. So can it be our lack of understanding of EQ stopping us from achieving all God wants us to be?

"Peace, I leave with you; My [perfect] peace I give to you; not as the world gives do I give to you. Do not let your heart be troubled, nor let it be afraid [Let My perfect peace calm you in every circumstance and give you courage and strength for every challenge]." (John 14:27 AMP). Inside of us is a place of peace that can only come from God—a place where it doesn't matter whether we have or don't have. Happiness doesn't come from things or people but rather from a place with God—I would call it the Garden of Eden—where worry and stress can't enter.

I can see how emotionally immature I was in my early years. My problem early on in my life was the suppressed, unprocessed emotions I buried in my heart. Let's take the word emotion and split it into e - motions which mean energy in motion. I recently learned that every feeling we experience should flow through us but what happens when emotions are not processed is that they entrap us in that moment and stay stored inside of our hearts therefore we never mature emotionally though outwardly we continue to grow. I call this frozen trauma if something happened to you when you were eight years old that part of you is frozen in time until you process the emotion. After the emotion is processed it is redeemed back to its current state of now. Later we will teach you how this works and reset back to your original settings.

I had succeeded in building a company, but my relationships with employees were horrible. I was a dictator and, ultimately, not a good leader. I had no emotional intelligence. My leadership was based on fear. However, I wasn't aware of myself! I didn't care about others' feelings, and I was self-driven. I was thirty-five years old with the emotional maturity of a ten-year-old. A ten-year-old is not mature or fully capable mentally of handling adult tasks, especially their emotional health, because they lack understanding, identity, and evolving.

I couldn't build a healthy working environment, which resulted from immaturity at a personal and emotional level. I needed to grow up emotionally. I was always looking for happiness outside myself, so I was often angry, and I would make sure everyone around me was also angry. I hurt people and created a work environment people dreaded going to, and the fuel to all this was my inability to process past emotions.

I can now see how much I have matured over the years, and this only happened when I became intentional about true happiness. Happiness is not always about becoming; it's about being. We often believe that happiness will occur when we become a big name in a particular professional field or attain a niche, house, or car. However, happiness can often come from us living in the present and being aware of the joys around us. We should stop and think about this for a second. Let's begin living in the present, this was a game-changer as I matured in EQ.

King David writes it this way "Be still, and know that I am God (Psalms 46:10 NIV). We can begin to apply this statement and enjoy "the now." To know God is to be in the now. This is where my emotions do not drive me; instead, I can better manage them. I choose to be in the now. I decided not to put my virtual reality glasses on and shoot to the future or the past but to remain in the now, where God wants to commune with you and me. The next chapters will teach tangible ways to implement this practice.

I remember going to the Dominican Republic with a few friends. Everyone wanted to go horseback riding, so I followed. Before we got on the horses, the staff trained us to manage the horses. These horses are powerful and dangerous, especially when people don't know how to handle them. I'm kind of a jokester, so I was in my own little world while the instructions were taught. One important thing they said was to wear long pants, but I wore shorts since I was not paying attention. When we moved toward the horses, my attitude was, "I've got this," but obviously I didn't. So, I was assigned to a horse, and we started moving when I got in line. Everything was good until my horse decided he wanted to run. Suddenly, he got out of the line and started going faster. I had no control as the horse's speed increased, and the horse ran quicker and quicker. I was all over the place. My legs were being scraped by the saddle, which was why long pants were required. The staff yelled, "Pull the reign! Pull the reign!" but I couldn't understand because of all the bouncing that was going on. What a mess I had created.

The manager pulled his horse up next to me, took the reins, and pulled it with all he had. I pulled too, and eventually, the horse halted. When I stopped and looked, I saw that the sides of my legs were scraped and bleeding because I hadn't worn the correct pants and did not listen to how to control the horse during training. What was supposed to be a joyful experience became a nightmare.

Our emotions are often similar. They will hurt us and others if we don't know how to control them. What's supposed to be a happy life becomes a nightmare, all because we can't control our emotions. We don't know how to pull the reins in and take control.

Things that Cripple Us

I was in the car business for over twenty-five years, and over the years, I became good at discerning what was wrong with a car by how it sounded. Every time I would take a car to the mechanic, he would ask what noise it was making, and after many years, I picked up the ability myself. By the sound of the car, I could determine the problem. I became so good at it that even though I am not in the car business anymore, if I get into a car and hear a noise, I can immediately tell what needs to be checked.

When I heard one of these noises and could determine the issue, all I had to do was buy the part that needed to be replaced. There were times when I couldn't resolve the problem by ear; I would go to a mechanic and he would pull out the big guns, which consisted of a $15,000 diagnostic computer. He would plug it into the car's computer and have the answer within minutes.

The mechanic would not start working on the car unless he could precisely identify the problem and replace that part to correct its sound. So it is with us; many times we don't activate discernment to see or hear the problems in our lives – that's the one reason why many people go to therapists. As they talk, the therapist listens to hear and pinpoint the issue. However, you can do this if you learn to listen, hear, and see yourself. Did you know we can do this? As mentioned before, Caroline Leaf calls it Multiple Perspective Advantage (MPA). In neuroscience, it is called metacognition. This method describes the ability to step back from oneself and watch and see one's actions from different angles to determine where they come from.

We were created, like God, to observe and be aware of our thoughts. No other being has this ability. We can selah (pause) between decisions! The apostle James says, "Know this, my beloved brothers let every person be quick to hear, slow to speak, slow to anger" (James 1:19 ESV). With practice and persistence, we will become experts in thought management. Someone who's emotionally intelligent is far superior to most. This will affect our careers, our relationships, and life as a whole.

In Romans 12:2 (NIV), Paul says that renewing the mind is like changing broken parts and exchanging one with another. According to this spiritual principle, renewing our minds is to renew our engines and transform our hearts. We will change into beings full of wholeness and complete not lacking anything. Our lives will be lives that sound good, the way God intended them to be. This will take time, effort, and persistence as we work on our hearts.

Take time during the day to listen and realize what area of your life needs changes in your heart. Every car has a check engine light to warn you something is wrong. The check engine light goes on in our lives when we experience pain. It can happen when you see someone or remember something from the past that hurt you. Your heart says, "There is something wrong that needs to be addressed." When we ignore the check engine lights of our hearts and leave those areas of pain, hurt, and trauma unattended, we are at risk of never living life as it was intended.

I was driving with my wife to a conference once, and the check engine light came on. She immediately advised me to pull over to see what was wrong. I insisted on waiting until later to address the problem. I didn't know that the car was running with no oil. Moments later, the vehicle shut down. We later found out the engine was seized, and the car was no good anymore because the engine was the heart of the car. So, it is with us. If we keep ignoring the signals from the heart, sooner or later, chaos erupts in our lives through sickness, emotional instability, and ill mental health. Unlike my car, for which I could buy a new engine, we can't buy a new heart.

This is a journey, not a sprint. It's a lifelong journey to reset all your settings to their original values. Don't be hard on yourself. Eventually, with practice, you'll become an excellent mechanic of the heart. There will be times you can't hear or see this, but these are the times you take out the big guns. A diagnostic computer functions like the Holy Spirit. When you tap in during your quiet time, present your cares to the Spirit of God within you. He has all the answers, and he'll give you a complete diagnostic and tell you where you need to change your mind and heart.

Effects of a Mismanaged Thought Life

In a groundbreaking study conducted by the American Medical Association, it was discovered that stress plays a significant role in approximately 90% of illnesses and diseases afflicting individuals today. This finding sheds light on the pervasive nature of stress and emphasizes the importance of understanding its purpose in our lives. A lack of EQ can cause us harm.

Contrary to popular belief, stress serves a fundamental purpose in our physiological and psychological well-being. It is an innate response designed to protect and prepare us for challenging situations. When faced with a perceived threat or demand, our bodies release stress hormones, such as adrenaline and cortisol, which trigger a cascade of physiological changes. These changes enable us to respond effectively to the situation at hand, enhancing our chances of survival and success.

However, when stress becomes chronic or overwhelming, it can have detrimental effects on our health. Prolonged exposure to stress hormones can disrupt various bodily systems, including the immune, cardiovascular, and nervous systems. This can lead to a host of physical and mental health problems, ranging from cardiovascular diseases and gastrointestinal disorders to anxiety and depression.

In ancient times long ago, there weren't any houses for protection. We lived in the wild. If a bear came along, we couldn't get away with saying, "Look how cute the bear is," or petting the bear; we needed to get out of the way. When fear sets in, it causes the body to release cortisol, a chemical released to mobilize fight or flight. After the bear is out of sight and the chaos has ceased, we don't continue with the mindset to run. Sometimes we can live our lives under the same mindset as if the bear is still chasing us, although the chase has passed. This is a mismanaged thought life that leads to disease.

In psychology, this mismanaged thought-life can be labeled post-traumatic stress disorder (PTSD). A typical example is someone goes to war, and when they come home, and the battle is long over, the mind is still in combat mode. Their mind still believes they are at war. The war is over, but the person's mind does not shut off. The body releases the chemicals needed to react to external signals of danger. But what happens when this reaction doesn't shut off? We stay stuck in our minds within the chaos of the past even though our surroundings are at peace. Also, while this is happening, you're telling the body by thought alone there is an imminent danger. This will cause the body to be supplied with energy to run and none to heal itself. The fight-or-flight response is not the proper reaction if you're not in a place of danger.

Guess what happens to your immune system during a stress reaction? The body is taking all its energy and putting it somewhere else. Imagine feeling your immune system shrink because you are stressed. You can't be stressed and peaceful at the same time. Peace allows us to access our creative nature, while stress can inhibit it. Stress is your chaotic nature. Chaos should not be the constant state in which we operate and live. We think and continue thinking of negative things. And guess what happens? You are signaling your body to "Run, Forrest, run," even though you are home. And that could be triggered by anyone or anything that has put stress in your life. You may look relaxed, but your mind is running. Why? You activated it with your thinking. We can take control of that with mind over matter.

The Genesis of Thought

Understand that you are not only reading. My words are air. You don't hear my words, but you are reading them. And somehow, something's happening in your brain right now. Something is being created that you can revisit later. Isn't that awesome? We are constantly creating. Our problem is retention. How do we retain things in our minds? It is by repetition. It is easy to maintain the hurt from the past, but it is hard to retain the promises of God for the future and live in the now.

Have you ever put something in storage, forgotten about it, and then found you've been paying sixty dollars monthly in storage fees for three or five years? You may then have realized you could have bought the item in storage thrice. But you were paying for storage for something that had no value in your life. It was losing value daily, and you kept it in your life as it continued depreciating.

So it is with our past emotional traumas we're paying to keep these stories in storage for experiences that lead to the development of unresolved emotions. These unresolved emotions, if not properly processed, can manifest as traumas that we carry with us into adulthood. The impact of these traumas can be significant, often causing us to dwell on the past and preventing us from moving forward in a healthy and positive way.

It is important to acknowledge that the negative events we experienced in our youth are a part of our personal history. However, we must also recognize that we have the power to separate these events from the negative emotions they have become associated with. By doing so, we can begin to break free from the chains of the past and live our lives in a more fulfilling and present manner.

In the realm of spiritual warfare, the scripture in 2 Corinthians 10:5 (ESV) instructs us to take every thought captive. This language of warfare implies the need for a battle plan, a strategic approach to dealing with the thoughts that enter our minds. When we take a thought captive, we must first question its origin and motives. Is it a thought from God? How does it make me feel? Is it a scheme of the enemy? Is it rooted in light or darkness? It is essential to discern the difference.

By taking a thought captive, we are essentially preventing it from taking control over our lives and hearts. This concept aligns with the wisdom shared in Proverbs 4:23 (NIV), which states, "Above all else, guard your heart, for everything you do flows from it." The thoughts we entertain have a profound impact on our actions and the course of our lives. Therefore, it becomes crucial to safeguard our hearts by carefully filtering the thoughts that enter our minds. By continuously practicing this you will continue to grow in your EQ.

Taking every thought captive requires discipline and discernment. It necessitates a deep understanding of God's Word and a sensitivity to the promptings of the Holy Spirit. As we engage in this spiritual battle, we must be vigilant in identifying thoughts that do not align with God's truth and purpose for our lives. By doing so, we can effectively combat the lies and deceptions that the enemy may seek to plant in our minds.

The battle plan for taking every thought captive involves actively engaging in prayer, meditating on Scripture, and seeking the guidance of the Holy Spirit. It requires a commitment to renewing our minds and aligning our thoughts with God's truth. Through this intentional process, we can break free from the strongholds of negative thinking, fear, and doubt. We can replace destructive thoughts with thoughts of faith, hope, and love.

In conclusion, taking every thought captive is a vital aspect of our spiritual journey. It empowers us to guard our hearts and align our minds with God's truth. By discerning the origin and motives of our thoughts, we can effectively combat the schemes of the enemy and walk in the freedom and victory that Christ has secured for us. In Hebrews 5:14 (NKJV) the writer states something profound. Let's read: "But solid food is for the mature, who by constant use have trained themselves to distinguish good and evil. This is primarily speaking about thoughts. Let us be steadfast in our commitment to this battle plan, for it holds the key to transforming our lives and experiencing the abundant life God has promised.

CHAPTER 9

PASSCODES AND PROGRAMS

Have you ever asked yourself, "Why do I think the way I think? Is it my parents' thinking, or is it my choosing? Am I hardwired this way for the rest of my life?"

The truth is that we are wired a certain way, but it is also true that our minds are malleable. This means we can put a new way of thinking on top of another one and feed it a positive thought. In our case, it is a positive thought full of life. If you do not feed the old, negative thoughts, sooner or later, they will become malnourished and will be pruned. Pruning in the neuroscience world occurs when one thought replaces another one. So, you can rewire old damaging emotional trauma and replace it with God's love. Changing your perspective of the event from hurt to compassion In our spiritual journeys, we know this process as renewing our minds. Will you forget the negative experiences that happened to you? No, you're going to remember them, but you will be able to reframe how you look at those experiences and change the emotions attached to them. That's fantastic news.

The invisible thought becomes visible by your will. I will say that again the invisible becomes visible making it something tangible. You have the power and the choice to create. We have the ability not only to create our future but also to create what we imagine. It becomes a magnet once you envision it. The creator created creation to create.

Let me share how you can change your perspective and re-code old programs. Here is an example, most people have access to a phone.

A passcode is needed to enter the phone. The passcode allows you to access the phone's main programs. But within the phone, there is another level of security to get personally secure information. The iCloud holds information such as credit card numbers and other personal information. There is one code to enter the phone's mainframe and another passcode to enter into personal settings so that you can access the information and change what needs to be changed.

We are similar! We might see someone from the past, and face recognition will act as a passcode that will bring up a file that stores information such as emotions, memories, and other impressions you relate to this person. Even if this person has similarities to traumas in your past this too will also activate programs. And here you go! In the blink of an eye, you can change how you feel because someone not only entered your phone but also entered into the secure programming.

After all, our lives are a collection of events, traumas, and situations, and people are attached to these collections. Someone may say something that reminds you of something your father said, and suddenly, the passcode has entered into the mainframe and pulled out a program of something that happened years ago. And not only do you remember that event, but you also feel the same way as if it happened just yesterday. Isn't it spine-chilling how we can see, hear, and smell something, and it can trigger an event that occurred over 15 years ago? Feeling the same way as you did when that particular situation took place. Now let's go deeper into understanding more about passcodes and programs.

Coding in computing is assigning a code to something for classification and identification. When you classify something, you set it aside in a library. And so, when you use a pass-code you bypass the code and enter into the program. That passcode brings out whatever information you classify. The passcode allows you to go into the program. The program is the event or the file that you're classifying. It can be a significant trauma or emotional event in your life. These events become the program. The passcode could be facial recognition. It could be their fingerprints or voice activation. Suppose the passcode is facial recognition. When you see the person, your mind is alerted that they are there, and the program causes the release of chemicals in your body. Then you feel anger, frustration, or fear. It can also occur for positive programs in our hearts. Whatever you feel, you just pulled up a program from the heart. The great news about this is that we can shift and change things. But again, if you are unaware of this, change might not happen very well.

Coding is using a programming language to get a computer to assimilate a program you desire. Every line of code tells a computer to do something. Similarly, everything that you look at is a signal. Signals go to your mind and then to your subconscious, searching for past experiences or similarities already inside your heart. That's how we discover whether we have things and situations that shouldn't be in our hearts.

We should ask questions such as the following:

- Why do I experience negative emotions when I see a particular person?
- What have I coded?
- What have I stored in my heart?
- What have I programmed in my heart that still affects me when I see that person?

The magic starts in step one awareness. The next step is the hard one. I often hear this: "I can't forgive someone. I don't know how to do it." I will teach you how to do it later in the book. I want you to remember that the experience will never change, but we can extract the negative emotion. We can't erase everything, but we can detach the emotional charge assigned to it. So, when you see someone who hurt you, it doesn't have to bring you back to the pain of the past. You can learn to react with compassion.

When you reprogram the old thing that happened to you in your life that hurt you, your reaction can be based on new programming. When that emotion comes up in your conscious mind, you have about fifteen minutes to deal with it, according to Dr. Caroline Leaf. However, it returns to your subconscious with a more hardened emotion if you do not deal with it. Even more stubborn to deal with when this emotion comes up the next time. Whether you believe it or not, it's what you do. We must improve at reprogramming things that come to our conscious mind the very instant we notice a disturbance.

A computer only functions as well as its coding and programming. Years ago, when you bought a new computer and turned it on, you looked at a black monitor. You had to format the hard drive and install an operating system to see something or even work with the computer. Now we know that the monitor is not the computer. It is only a screen that displays what is inside the computer. What you see on the screen is the inside of your hard drive. It's the coding and programming that makes the whole package work. – Therefore, if, for example, you have a virus on your hard drive, this will not change by turning on and off the monitor. You need to change what is inside the computer.

Like us, behavior modification is not going to get you there. Behavior modification is only an outward change that is temporary and does not last. There must be a hard-drive correction. When someone presses your buttons, there's an area inside your heart you need to deal with. Maybe you have some insecurity, or perhaps you're battling with low self-esteem. These are the things you must question. You have to examine your program. "Why am I feeling this? Where does it come from?" We must uproot things that are not yielding in our lives. We have to go to the roots and pull it out. If you cut it in half, there won't be long-lasting change; it will only be a temporary behavior modification. In other words, withholding feelings without addressing the core problem causes the suffering we don't have to live with. This is what we want to change.

The code in our internal programs is spiritual. The code is what allows the information that's in our subconscious to be brought to our conscious. The program is everything that's in the subconscious or history. Only through our spiritual awareness of these programs can we address and alter the codes from which they arise.

The apostle Paul said in 1 Corinthians 2:14 (VOICE), "But a person who denies spiritual realities will not accept the things that come through the Spirit of God; they all sound foolish. He cannot grasp them because they are disseminated, discerned, and valued by the Spirit." Even Jesus says in Matthew 13:14 (NLT), "When you hear what I say, you will not understand. When you see what I do, you will not comprehend." People won't comprehend or understand the work God is doing if they perceive it from their everyday consciousness. We have to proceed with discernment from the spiritual realm. The Spirit of God in our hearts is our tutor, teacher, and revealer.

Think about going to a 3-D movie. If no one gave you 3-D glasses, you could not perceive the film correctly because you need 3-D glasses to view it. 3-D glasses allow you to see things deeper. The term "3-D" means "three-dimensional." You see a 3-D film in a dimension you can't see with the naked eye. And the Holy Spirit acts as our 3-D glasses. You must make sure you have the glasses on so you can see and discern everything with a spiritual sense and awareness. You have to perceive it with the eyes of God. You have to see it through the Spirit of God. True freedom occurs inside. When we can't see clearly and discern what we are feeling, ask in prayer, "Holy Spirit, reveal your truth to me."

Scripture reminds us of the profound truth that our hearts can be deceitful above all else. Jeremiah 17:9 (KJV) states, "The heart is deceitful above all things and desperately wicked; Who can know it?" This verse serves as a reminder that there are mysteries within our hearts that may elude our understanding. Often, we may believe that we have moved on from certain experiences or emotions, only to find that they are still lingering deep within our hearts. It is crucial to recognize that when negative emotions resurface in our conscious mind, they may not necessarily be directly related to the present moment or the person involved. Instead, they may stem from past hurts or pains that have yet to be fully addressed.

In such instances, we may find ourselves reacting with intensity to a situation or person, unaware that our response is fueled by unresolved emotions from the past. It is important to acknowledge and accept these negative emotions that arise from our past experiences. By doing so, we can begin the process of healing and growth. Dealing with these emotions from their root is essential. It requires a conscious effort on our part to confront and process the emotions that have been left unattended. In doing so, we can prevent them from influencing our present relationships and circumstances. In the following sections, I will provide guidance on how to effectively deal with these emotions and address them at their core. It is crucial to be aware of our emotions and make a continuous effort to process them, ensuring our emotional well-being and personal growth.

Whatever thoughts you value most will eventually be downloaded as a program into your heart, whether it's good or bad. That's why you must be an inner engineer and focus on your thoughts. Look at an umpire; his job is to keep an eye on what? Come on, baseball lovers. His job is to keep his eye on the ball. He is watching to see whether it is a foul or a strike.

We must "umpire" our thoughts to ensure we know where they're coming from, whether negative or positive.

Suppressed emotions are like old information on an overloaded computer. We have no space for new information unless we delete or move to trash. Jesus taught us that we cannot put new wine into old wineskins (See Mark 2:22 NLT). This reminds us that we must re-code our programs so they can display His grace on the screens of our lives. Too much unnecessary information slows down the whole system. What good is buying a new shiny computer if we bog it down with old files (past) and slow it down with unnecessary negative emotionally charged memories?

Files that are moved to the recycle bin (on Windows PCs), or the trash (on Macs) stay in those folders until they are emptied. However, they can still be retrieved with the right software once deleted or emptied. We want to arrive at a place where the only things we want to recover from our past are the lessons that benefit our present. You are learning this so that you can put it into action. When deleting files, you're not going to forget the situation, but you will delete the emotional charge attached to that person and see him or her with compassion.

Memorization, not just hearing, is part of learning. Memorization is how we download new programs into our hearts. If you don't memorize something, you can never remember it because it was not properly stored in your long-term memory. You only remember something you will have allocated as necessary, have spent time on, or have an emotional charge attached to it. This is the process of taking something and making it a long-term memory. It doesn't stay in our short-term memory (mind); it has to go to our long-term memory (subconscious), a three-step process. The three-step process takes sixty-three days, according to Dr. Caroline Leaf. We accept new information into our hearts to replace the old with the new.

1. You destroy your old thinking by meditating on new information for twenty-one days.
2. Then, over the next twenty-one days, you disrupt your old way of thinking and establish a new one,
3. Lastly, it is permanently downloaded in the following twenty-one days.

That's sixty-three days to create a habit, and you have now installed a new way of thinking.

Programmers

Parents have an incredible responsibility in shaping the foundation of their children's lives. Just like programmers, they have the power to determine what gets imprinted in their young minds during those crucial first seven years. It is during this time that the programs they instill become ingrained in their subconscious, influencing their beliefs, self-worth, and potential.

Imagine the impact of positive programming! If parents nourish their children with love, encouragement, and belief in their abilities, they set them up for greatness. By instilling confidence and reminding them of their worth, parents empower their children to chase their dreams and achieve extraordinary things.

Unfortunately, the opposite can also hold true. Negative programming, such as constantly belittling or degrading a child, can create a corrupt program. Words like "worthless," "you'll never be anything good," or "you're ugly" etch deep into their subconscious, paving the way for self-sabotage and limiting beliefs. Many of us have experienced this but fortunately, it can stop with us and we can positively impact the next generation.

But fear not! It is never too late to rewrite these programs and guide our children toward a brighter future. We must remember the wisdom shared in the scriptures about leading a child in the right way. By nurturing their potential, teaching them kindness and compassion, and instilling positive values and God's word, we can help them overcome any negative programming and ensure they don't deviate from the path of success and fulfillment.

Let us embrace the power we hold as parents, not only as programmers but as architects of our children's lives. Let's make sure our programs are updated to reflect Jesus. Let us build a strong foundation, brick by brick, with love, kindness, and encouragement. Together, we can empower our children to become the best versions of themselves, unleashing their limitless potential and paving the way for a future filled with greatness.

Re-programming

I looked up the word "remember." It pertains to bringing to one's mind an awareness of someone or something that one has seen, known, or experienced. So, to remember is to bring to mind something that is already part of you. If you're a member of something, you are a part of that thing.

Meditate on His Word Day and night; that's what the Bible says, so it can be part of who you are. "And you shall know the truth, and the truth shall free you" (John 8:32 NKJV). The Bible says, "Know the truth." In Greek, the word for know is "ginosko" (to become one). So, we have to take the Word of God and allow it to be in our hearts as a member of who we are; that's why I say when I meditate on something, "That word is mine." It's me; it is who I am. It is not just a part of me, but there's a process to becoming one with the word. We have to program his words in our hearts.

John 3:16 (NLT) can be seen as a code, but what it means to you is the program. Meditating on the first part of John 3:16 is not just "for God so loved the world." We can program it to be, "God so loved me that he gave his son. God loves me; I'm God's special possession. I am his." This is the expansion of John 3:16. It's the program. Don't just memorize a verse; establish the significance and apply the Word he is speaking directly to you. Elevate your emotions as if God himself was speaking to you. When you start thinking and meditating on scripture, you allow God to open up about what it means to you. Even a download from a computer takes time. If you're downloading an app, you must wait until it is downloaded before you can open it up. When you're meditating on the scripture, John 3:16, you're chewing on it, so to speak. Have you ever eaten something so good that you just kept chewing on it as if you didn't want to swallow it because you just wanted to savor it forever? That's what you do with the Word. Savor John 3:16. Allow the expansion of the program.

This meditation will allow the Word of God to be in our hearts. We become inner programmers. If we can't get the Word of God in our hearts, it won't produce in our lives. For this, you must be disciplined, and you must put in the time. If you want to meditate in the morning, maybe you can get up a half hour earlier than usual. Perhaps you would like to meditate at night before you go to sleep. These moments are the best times for learning and programming because in the morning and at night, you're more susceptible to receiving what you're listening to. Many people go to sleep listening to meditative music along with scripture. Why? It allows it to penetrate the heart. If we can't get the Word of God into our hearts, then it doesn't give us the ability to shift or change our perception of the world. Proverbs 4:20 (NIV) says, "My son, pay attention to what I say; turn your ear to my words. Do not let them out of your sight. Keep them within your heart; for they are life." Notice it does not say "into your mind"; it has to penetrate deeper and be hardwired into your heart.

In the book of Numbers, the Bible says that God told the Israelites they were going into the Promised Land. God said this—not a man or a prophet, but God himself. But when they went into the Promised Land, what happened? There were twelve of them; ten of them saw giants, and two saw grasshoppers. The two people who saw grasshoppers, Joshua and Caleb, saw that the God who promised them was more significant than the obstacles before them.

Were they looking at the same scenario? Of course, they were looking at the same scene. But one was looking at it through the natural lens, and the other two were looking at what God can do through the spiritual lens of his word. What they looked at is small compared to the big God they serve. God must be part of who you are in your heart. If the Word was in their hearts, they would have seen grasshoppers instead of giants. Jacob and Caleb believed in God's Word. The word was memorized in their heart; it was not from their natural sense or reasoning but rather through the lenses of God.

We must get good at blocking negative thoughts. We can better adjust the negative things in our hearts and start shifting them when we are aware. You will learn how to better deal with these negative thoughts by working on them every time something surges up. We can't allow our thoughts to run our lives.

In the realm of personal growth and self-development, an important aspect often overlooked is the management of our emotions. This is an ongoing habit. Just like my horse story spoken about previously, our emotions possess the potential to shape the course of our lives if left uncontrolled. It is imperative, therefore, that we recognize the reins of control we possess and steer our thoughts in the direction of positivity and growth. Consider the impact of our unaddressed negative thoughts on the generations to come. Our children, and their children after them, deserve an inheritance that transcends material wealth. They deserve an emotional landscape devoid of the giants we failed to conquer. By taking charge of our own emotional well-being, we can ensure that our descendants inherit a legacy of inner strength and resilience.

It is within our power to break the cycle and prevent the negative thoughts and unprocessed negative emotions that plague us from becoming the burden of future generations. Let us not allow our children's inheritance to be tainted by the unresolved issues we neglect to confront. Instead, let us embark on a journey of self-discovery and emotional mastery, so that we may pave the way for a brighter and more fulfilling future.

The ASV version of Ephesians 4:27 says, "Neither gives place to the devil." It's almost like if someone knocks on your door and you let them sit in your house; you're giving them a place. The person knocked on the door, you opened the door, and he sat in your house. You allowed him a space, although he was not welcomed. Think about this. What strangers would we allow a place in our lives? If the answer is no one, then why are we allowing the devil's negative thoughts permanent residence in our lives? Every day the enemy is knocking, and every day a negative emotion is trying to take over your soul; it is trying to take over how you feel. When we allow the enemy access to our mind his main goal is to become a negative program.

An antivirus program on a computer is designed to eliminate all viruses. If you open an email with a virus, it is on your computer! So, think of an email as a thought. Once you open it up because you don't know where it was sent from, you open it to a realm that allows the virus to destroy your computer. What is there to destroy? Your computer, which metaphorically is your heart. Don't let the virus in. If you expose yourself, you're giving it a foothold. You can give coronavirus a foothold by being around people who are infected. Why? Because you never know where it is. It is something in the air. You might tell yourself, "Well, I don't know how I caught it." You were exposed to it. You allowed the virus in. You gave it a foothold, and now it's in your system. Once there, it destroys from the inside. Now you are trying to fix something inside your heart after you allowed it entry.

Deuteronomy 30:19 (NIV) says, "This day, I call the heavens and the earth as witnesses against you that I have set before your life and death, blessings, and curses. Now choose life, so that you and your children may live". Life is full of choices. When we choose to work on old programs and establish new ones, by being intentional, we not only redirect our lives but also the lives of those around us. The choices we make get passed on, because whatever you establish can influence the codes and programming we pass on to the next generation.

CHAPTER 10

THE ART OF HARPU

In Hebrew, the word "Harpu" means to be still. I love how Google defines it as "Be still" or "Hush" or "Shut up!" I would have to imagine the "Shut up!" translation is one of those situations we see in the movies where someone slaps their best friend to get them to calm down and re-center. This chapter is for the understanding that mindfulness and meditation originated from scripture and God called it stillness. God speaks to us in the book of Psalms, stating something profound that revolutionized my thinking.

Be still and know that I am God.
I will be exalted among the nations,
I will be exalted on the earth! (Psalms 46:10 ESV)

Strong's Lexicon defines "still" as "be still, relax, to sink down, let drop, be disheartened or to withdraw." Mindfulness pertains to being in the now. It implies disconnecting from all things. You're neither harboring yesterday nor anxiously premeditating for the future. When we practice mindfulness, we bring all our awareness to the present moment. I am not my title; I disconnect from all things to be present in the now with God.

In this section, I would like to debunk some untrue notions about mindfulness and meditation. Just in the last few years, I have come to realize and understand this is key to discovering your inner kingdom. But before I go there, let me share some wisdom on the anatomy of the mind and where you will grow with the art of Harpu. The theory is that people are either left-brained or right-brained, meaning that one side of the brain is dominant. If you're primarily analytical and methodical in your thinking, which most of us are, you're said to be left-brained. You're considered right-brained if you tend to be more creative or artistic. Most neuroscientists state that around 90 percent of people are left-brained, and only 10 percent are right-brained. Do you see the problem? Paul, one of Jesus's disciples, called the five senses the carnal mind, which meant the mind of the flesh or reasoning, and now science corroborates this by calling it logical thinking. "For those who live according to the flesh set their minds on the things of the flesh, but those who live according to the Spirit, set sight of things of the Spirit. For to be carnally minded is death, but to be spiritually minded is life and peace" (Romans 8:5–6 ESV).

Did you know that the right brain develops first? It does so until children are three to four years of age. This is the innocent stage, during which children believe all. On the other hand, the left brain doesn't come to awareness until children are approximately seven years old; hence the first seven years are recognized as a critical period in child development. You may have even heard the term "golden brain," referring to people who use both sides of their brains equally. As our inner self grows, let's become golden!

What would it look like if we were 50 percent left-minded and 50 percent right-minded—with the imaginative and creative parts of our minds working in tandem with our logical and analytical minds? This is where the art of Harpu helps us to transform. This would take humanity to another level. We would see the church moving in a new dimension that Jesus calls heaven on earth! We are called to walk by faith and not by sight (2 Corinthians 5:7 ESV), and then we are shown in Hebrews 11:1–3 that it is by faith that we come to understand spiritual things. This faith is a function of our right brain, demonstrating that we must learn the functions of spirit to operate in the heaven-on-earth reality.

Mindfulness and meditation are sometimes treated as out-of-this-world things that we should have no part in unless we want to be seen as strange hippies. But the inverse is true. Mindfulness in its simplicity is awareness. In the case of the Tower of Babel (Genesis 11), we observe self-gratification and the self-god, Mr. Ego. If we see the story of the Tower of Babel, they used their imagination to create a tower to reach heaven, but God stopped them because the purpose was for their gain. Anything we build apart from God's plan is in vain. But when we use God's plan to help and develop others, we operate in the realm of purpose. Meditation is good when used in the right way.

Mindfulness can be described as being present with God. This "now" serves as the bridge to meditation. Meditation is your focused attention on one thing—whether it's scripture, God himself, love, or joy—just focusing on what it is. It is a posture that leans into the present surroundings and thoughts and rests in the moment. But the only way you get there is through the bridge called mindfulness, being aware of the present moment "now", It's the best way I can explain it.

Mindfulness, often misunderstood, holds a significant place in our lives. It is crucial to dispel the misconceptions surrounding this practice and recognize its true potential. Contrary to popular belief, mindfulness is not confined to the solitude of our homes but rather extends to all aspects of our daily existence. It is not solely about slowing down; instead, mindfulness empowers us to enhance our cognitive processes and maximize our effectiveness in various endeavors. By embracing mindfulness, we open ourselves to a world of possibilities and embark on a journey towards unparalleled achievements.

One misconception about mindfulness is that it is a private affair, limited to personal reflection and contemplation. While individual practice is indeed integral, mindfulness also encourages us to apply its principles in our interactions with others and in the pursuit of our goals. Whether it be in the workplace, relationships, or personal growth, mindfulness equips us with the tools to navigate challenges, make informed decisions, and cultivate a state of heightened awareness.

Another prevalent misconception is that mindfulness is solely about slowing down, adopting a leisurely pace, and disconnecting from the demands of modern life. While it is true that mindfulness encourages us to embrace moments of stillness and introspection, it is equally focused on optimizing our mental processes to operate at a heightened level of efficiency. By cultivating mindfulness, we enhance our ability to concentrate, remain present, and make conscious choices, enabling us to accomplish tasks with greater effectiveness and precision.

It is worth noting that mindfulness is not a new concept; its roots can be traced back to ancient philosophies and spiritual traditions. Jesus practiced mindfulness and meditation, he often retrenched alone to be still with the Father.

It is essential to recognize the true essence of mindfulness and dispel the misconceptions that surround it. By embracing mindfulness as a comprehensive practice that extends beyond the boundaries of our homes, we unlock the key to personal growth, enhanced productivity, and a more fulfilling existence. Let us embark on this journey of self-discovery and harness the power of mindfulness to propel ourselves to unprecedented heights of success and fulfillment.

Harpu is all about mindfulness and being still. We have an attention muscle that allows us to be on task with what we're doing when it's focused. It is us with all our hearts and minds. It's slowing down the mind so it can connect with the heart. This is the essence of Harpu; it is oneness, in the moment, and in stillness. One thing that challenged me for a long time is when the writer of Hebrews 4:11 (KJV) states "Let us labor therefore to enter into that rest, lest any man falls after the same example of unbelief." Notice how he says labor to enter. When we think of labor we think of work which is the opposite of rest. I have learned that in order to enter into rest I have to pay attention and concentrate on my present now. This takes effort. It's consciously disconnecting from my outer world to connect to my inner world. Therefore, it takes work on our behalf to enter into his rest.

Earlier in the book, I mentioned that our minds process about fifty bits of information per second. Our subconscious processes information at one thousand times that speed. This is what happens when the mind and heart operate cohesively it speeds up. Richard Davidson, a neuroscientist at the University of Wisconsin, names "focus" as one of a handful of essential life abilities, each based on a separate neural system, that guides us through the turbulence of our inner lives, our relationships, and whatever challenges life brings.

Research shows that our minds wander about 50 percent of the time and that when our minds wander, we are never as happy as when our minds are in the present moment. If your mind is in the future, worrying about something that's going to happen, or in the past because you regret something, you're more likely to feel more negative emotions. But you'll feel happier when you're in the present moment, in the now, even if you're doing a task you don't particularly like. You'll be more productive in that state because you will naturally be focused and flowing with a higher source—God. Focusing on one thing at a time will help us do that one thing well in less time. This is why we call it an art with practice you can master stillness.

Mindfulness allows us to shift our relationship to our present experience. Instead of getting pulled into negative emotions or thoughts (which is what happens when we're depressed or anxious), we see them as simply thoughts, and that disempowers them. Research at UCLA shows that when you can name a feeling, such as, "I'm feeling depressed again," you shift the activity levels neurologically from the part of the brain that is depressed to the part of the brain that is happy. This can diminish depression and enhance your ability to understand it or see it as just a feeling. If you read 2 Corinthians 10:4–5, you will realize what is today labeled as "spiritual warfare" is in the mind. Paul writes, "The weapons of the war we're fighting are not of this world but are powered by God and effective at tearing down the strongholds erected against His truth. We are demolishing arguments and ideas, every high-and-mighty philosophy that pits itself against the knowledge of the one true God. "We are taking prisoners of every thought, every emotion, and subduing them into obedience to the Anointed One" 2 Corinthians 10:4–5 (VOICE). When we actively engage not to be mindless but to be mindful in our mind, we suddenly open ourselves up to the possibility of finally overcoming our greatest enemy—our thoughts!

Mindfulness is awareness. It is noticing and paying attention to thoughts, feelings, behaviors, and everything else. Mindfulness can be practiced at any time, wherever we are, whomever we are with, and whatever we do by showing up and fully engaging in the here and now. That means being free of both the past and future (the what-ifs and maybes) and free of judgment of right or wrong (the I'm-the-best and I'm-no-good scenarios) so that we can be present without distraction. This is key! Mindfulness is the awareness that arises when we nonjudgmentally pay attention to the present moment.

Mindfulness cultivates access to core aspects of our minds and bodies that our sanity depends on. It includes tenderness and kindness toward us and restores the dimensions of our beings. These have never been missing, but we haven't been experiencing them because we have been absorbed elsewhere. When your mind clarifies and opens, your heart also clarifies and opens. This is called mind-and-heart coherence. It's when the two become one, in harmony, where the magic begins. "Happy chemicals" are activated in the brain that can lower blood pressure, improve digestion, and relax tension around areas of pain. When there's no harmony between mind and heart it's called incoherence, out of order.

Mindfulness is simple to practice but extraordinary in its effect. It's as if I found a new life when I started to practice mindfulness and meditation. This is not a bad deal, considering that all that is needed is to pay attention, which sounds like something we should all be doing but often forget to do. When we do pay attention, then change becomes possible.

Meditation changes us, as it returns us to our right mind. Mindfulness and meditation are mirror-like reflections of each other; mindfulness supports and enriches meditation, while meditation nurtures and expands mindfulness. Where mindfulness can be applied to any situation throughout the day, meditation is usually practiced for a specific amount of time.

Mindfulness and meditation are two practices that have gained significant attention in recent years, as people seek ways to find inner peace and reduce stress in their lives. While these terms are often used interchangeably, there are subtle differences between them.

Mindfulness can be defined as the conscious awareness of the present moment, without judgment or attachment. It involves being fully present in the here and now, paying attention to your thoughts, feelings, and sensations without getting caught up in them. By cultivating mindfulness, individuals can develop a greater sense of clarity and focus, as well as an increased ability to manage their emotions.

On the other hand, meditation refers to a specific technique or practice that allows individuals to enter a state of deep relaxation and heightened awareness. It involves focusing the mind on a particular object, such as the breath, in order to quiet the incessant chatter of thoughts and achieve a state of inner calm. Through regular meditation practice, individuals can experience a sense of profound stillness and connection to a deeper aspect of themselves.

While mindfulness serves as a bridge to the meditative state, it is through the practice of meditation that one truly enters the realm of nothingness. In meditation, one transcends the boundaries of the self and becomes one with the present moment, free from identification with thoughts, emotions, or external distractions. This state of selflessness and pure awareness is often described as a state of bliss, where the noise of the world fades away and one becomes fully immersed in the present moment to hear from God.

It is important to note that meditation is not about forcefully pushing away thoughts or trying to empty the mind. Rather, it is about cultivating focused attention and allowing thoughts to come and go without attachment or judgment. By observing thoughts without getting caught up in them, one can experience a sense of spaciousness and tranquility.

Many of our thoughts are heavily loaded with negative emotions. If you don't touch them, if you don't do anything with them, and if you don't get caught in them, they self-liberate, naturally, into awareness. This awareness is like touching a soap bubble. You know, it's fun to touch it and watch it pop. But even if you don't touch it, you can still see it float to the sky and watch it go poof all by itself. Sit down and begin to watch your thoughts. You'll see this is not rocket science. You don't have to sit in a cave for thirty years to have this kind of experience. All you need to do, in a sense, is get out of your way. Now, I'm not saying that's easy. It can be challenging. But you can have moments when you get out of your way. Remember this, you are conditioning your body to something new, let's be patient.

Meditation practices can help you observe your mind and become aware of and recognize its tendencies. It tends to wander, but the mind can help you through that awareness. It shifts your attention back to the present moment. Meditation is an exercise in which you fully engage with the present moment. So it's a fantastic way to train your mind to be more present with current events. There is a novel by Aldous Huxley called Island, written in his later years when he became very interested in spiritual teachings. It tells the story of a man shipwrecked on a remote island, cut off from the rest of the world. This island contains a unique civilization. The unusual thing about it is that its inhabitants, unlike the rest of the world, are sane. The man notices the colorful parrots perched in the trees, and they seem to be constantly croaking the words "Attention. Here and now. Attention. Here and now. Attention." We later learn that the islanders taught them these words to be reminded continually to stay present.

I wish for you to see meditation as an exercise and a practice. When we think about these two words, they lead us away from self-condemnation and perfectionism. No one is perfect at the art of meditation. Even monks who meditate throughout the day see meditation as a practice. We get better at it through practice. It's considered an exercise because we get stronger mentally as we practice it daily. So please don't beat yourself up. If one day you meditate for five minutes, while on others, you might be able to do twenty-five. The goal is to practice daily.

Countless times I tried to go into prayer with transparency and vulnerability, only to fall into the chaos of repeated thoughts. My day repeats itself through the thoughts of insignificant things I can't control, only to bring me into a place of frustration.

Jesus taught us that we couldn't add a single hour to our lives through worry (Matthew 6:27 NIV) and, in this same chapter, stated, "Do not worry about tomorrow" (Matthew 6:34 NIV), because he fully understands the current struggles of today's generation. Have you ever been there? Have you ever wanted to talk to God but somehow, The world's chaos and chatter wouldn't stop?

God says, "Be still and know that I am God" (Psalm 46:10 NIV). This means we become still as we focus on God and his goodness and allow ourselves to slow down. Slowing down and breathing slowly will enable the body to come to a place that allows the mind to be still. As we concentrate and focus our attention on one thing, the brain begins to work its magic. Our energy rests in that one thing, and when in meditation, it shuts down the chatterbox of our day's worries. It's just you and God. Mindfulness becomes a bridge that brings us to reflection. This bridge leads into a world of focus, joy, and peace.

On any one day, there are moments when nothing is going on, but we link up what is happening from thought to thought without any space. We overlook the spaciousness that it's all happening and end up with a day full of worry, toxicity, and stress. This space can be for peace and joy or anxiety and stress. Mostly though, we let our minds go to the negativity around us. We have the option. What will you choose? Would you prefer peace and joy obtained through mindfulness and meditation or anxiety and stress from ruminating over endless thoughts?

Nowadays, mindfulness and meditation often mean the same thing, which can be confusing. Here's my simple version: meditation can take on diverse forms. Some aim to develop a clear, focused mind, known as "Clear Mind" meditations. Others seek to develop altruistic states, such as loving-kindness, compassion, and forgiveness, known as "Open Heart" meditations. Others use the body to build awareness, and repetition of scripture, as you know, is what becomes etched in our hearts. I pray that the secret of joy will not be missing until you are in your older years. Make the art of stillness a practice, and your older years will instead be a time to testify of all the joys of presence.

Pay careful attention to the following statement. If you do mindfulness practice for ten minutes a day (or if you're feeling up for a challenge, you can do it for ten minutes three times a day), something remarkable happens to your attention. Multitasking will become a thing of the past. People, on average, look at their email about fifty times a day. They look at their Facebook pages twenty times a day, and that's just the tip of the iceberg. There's also Instagram and phone calls; whatever they have, they must do. What this means for attention is that focus is an endangered species. Attention then goes to the most significant opportunity or threat we perceive in our environment.

Where our attention goes, our emotions follow. Say there's something like a dark shadow moving. Your attention will go to that shadow automatically. The reason that we have attention is to pay attention, and then we can summon all our resources to either take advantage of the opportunity or avoid the threat. That's the purpose of attention. We block everything out and focus on one thing at a particular moment. This item is of the highest value or, potentially, the greatest threat. There's so much happening in our lives that we pay attention to, and quite frankly, the little devices we carry around don't help much because they absorb our attention.

Mindfulness meditation is a form of clear-mind meditation. During mindfulness meditation, attention is paid to the natural rhythm of the breath while sitting or slowly walking over a bridge. This focused attention allows the neurons to quiet down from chaos to calm. It is like a conductor stopping all the instruments at one time. This alone can have an enormous impact. Ultimately, this method is simply an aid, not the experience itself. A hammer can help build a house, but it's not the house.

In the same way, meditation practice is not an end in itself. We may wander off thinking of other things, but stillness will always be there because we have practiced meditation. It is a companion to have throughout life, like an old friend we turn to when needing direction, inspiration, and clarity. There's no right or wrong way to practice; we all do it differently. Most important of all, however, meditation is to be enjoyed; it's to be in the presence of God.

We have learned quite a lot about the effects of long-term meditation in people like monks who meditate for fifty thousand hours in their lifetimes. Studies show that this completely changes the electrophysiological responses of their brains. They have much higher levels of gamma waves, which is a particular frequency of waves. This can boost your immune system, lower your blood pressure, and help you deal with various problems, including irritable bowel syndrome and psoriasis.

A study from Harvard shows that short daily doses of meditation can grow the gray matter in critical areas of your brain related to self-awareness and compassion and shrink the gray matter in the area associated with stress. We all need peace of mind, right? Peace of mind can come from mindfulness. Through that, we understand how kindness, compassion, presence, and focus are all summed up in the now.

The best time for practicing mindful meditation is in the morning, as we awaken from our slumber, our brain waves slowly transition from the deep and restful delta state to the more alert and active beta state. It's like shifting gears in a manual vehicle, gradually building up momentum as we move through the different gears.

Just like starting in first gear (Delta), we begin our day in a state of calmness and tranquility. Our minds are clear, our thoughts are focused, and we are ready to embark on a brand-new day. As the morning progresses and the world around us comes alive, our brain waves shift to the second gear (Theta), preparing us for the tasks and challenges that lie ahead.

With each passing hour, our brain waves ascend to higher and faster frequencies, just like shifting gears in a car. We reach the third gear (Alpha), where our minds become more engaged, alert, and creative. Here is the place I call the God zone. It's the best place to be mindful and stay a while, practice gratitude, and focus on God and his greatness. Finally, we reach the fourth gear (Beta), where we are at our peak performance. Our brain waves are in the beta state, fully awake and ready to conquer whatever comes our way. We are focused, energized, and operating at our optimum capacity.

But just as a car must eventually come to a stop, our brain waves must also wind down. As the night approaches, we gradually shift from the fourth gear (Beta) to the third (Alpha). Again the aim is to stop for a while here and practice mindfulness and meditation, then the second (Theta), and eventually as the night progresses we go back to the first gear (Delta). Our minds start to slow down, preparing for a peaceful and rejuvenating night's sleep.

This beautiful rhythm of shifting brain waves mirrors the ebb and flow of life itself. It reminds us that every day is a new opportunity to evolve, grow, and reach our full potential. It reminds us that there are times to accelerate and times to decelerate and that finding balance and harmony is essential for our well-being.

So, as you go about your day, remember the symphony of brain waves within you. Embrace the gradual transition from delta to beta, and savor the unique experiences that each gear brings. And at night, as you wind down and shift into lower gears, let go of the day's worries and find solace in the peacefulness of the delta state.

You have the power to harness the energy of your brain waves, tap into your true potential, and create a life that is in perfect harmony with the rhythm of God. Embrace the journey, my friend, and let your brain waves guide you to greatness.

Life is not perfect and may never be perfect. But how much effort do we put into trying to be perfect? Humans are trying to figure out the most effective ways to be human. Patience is a beautiful quality to have. So, on those days full of stress, challenging people, and situations, take some time and practice the 4-7-8 breathing method from Dr. Andrew Weil, MD, to enter homeostasis to become one mind, body, and soul to shift into lower heavenly gears.

Follow the steps below to see how you can practice 4-7-8 breathing. You can do this anywhere and anytime, as long as you are present. When you are starting, begin with practicing twice a day. Go through the cycle of inhaling for four seconds, holding your breath for seven seconds, and exhaling for eight seconds. Do this for four cycles in a row. As your lungs develop, you can increase to eight cycles. This is when you are considered an expert. Beginners can practice for four cycles, and intermediate practitioners for six cycles. High-five yourself for your achievement

1. Find a comfortable place to sit up with your back straight.
2. Place your tongue against the back of your top teeth and keep it there.
3. Exhale completely through your mouth, around your tongue, making a whooshing sound. Purse your lips if it helps.
4. Close your lips and inhale through your nose for a count of four.
5. Hold your breath for a count of seven seconds.
6. Exhale completely through your mouth, making a whooshing sound for a count of eight seconds.
7. This completes one cycle. Repeat for three more cycles.

This technique has been a game-changer in my life. It is like training wheels once your body gets conditioned it becomes autonomous. For many years, I had a problem going into prayer because of the chatterbox in my mind. Once I mastered this practice, I could use it whenever I needed to be in harmony with myself. It will become more rewarding as you use it. Practice breathing before you respond to any stressful situation and whenever you cannot get to sleep.

Mindful breathing can release oxytocin to calm your mind and allow you to enter a state of peace. Within your body, you have a natural stress response designed to help you deal with dangerous situations. This fight-or-flight response can help you survive but can affect your health when overused for everyday stressors.

This stress response suppresses your immune system and can cause other health problems, including high blood pressure, depression, and anxiety. The relaxation response interrupts this stress response with a profound sense of rest.

The sympathetic nervous system controls your body's stress response. The parasympathetic nervous system controls your body's rest response.

When you activate one of these, you suppress the other. This is why deep breathing is so effective at causing the relaxation response. The 4-7-8 breathing technique is one deep breathing method that you can use to reap all these benefits. However, the particular method you use doesn't matter. You can try another breathing exercise if the 4-7-8 process doesn't work for you. You should experience the relaxation response with any breathing method that is slow and deep.

Just be patient. Just be. Just do.

CHAPTER 11

HARPU DAY AND NIGHT PRACTICE

Welcome, dear reader, to chapter 11 a journey of self-discovery and transformation. Today, we embark on a path that will lead us to the profound depths of our minds, where true change begins. Prepare yourself to learn, unlearn, and relearn, for these are the stepping stones to a life filled with joy and purpose.

Imagine your mind as a vast ocean, constantly churning with thoughts, ideas, and beliefs. In order to navigate this sea of consciousness, we must first learn to quiet the waves. Find a moment of stillness in your day, a sanctuary where you can retreat from the noise and chaos of the world. In this stillness, you will find the key to unlocking your true potential.

As you immerse yourself in silence, allow your thoughts to settle like the sediment at the bottom of a calm lake. Breathe deeply, inhaling peace and exhaling tension. In this serene state, you will discover the power to download new programs into your heart. These programs are the seeds of change, waiting to sprout and blossom within you.

But remember, dear reader, that knowledge without application is like a bird without wings. Absorb these principles into the very fabric of your being. Let them permeate your thoughts, actions, and intentions. Embrace them with fervor, for it is through the application of these principles that true transformation occurs.

Now, let us delve into the three levels of achieving change. First, we must learn. We must acquire new knowledge, explore different perspectives, and expand our understanding of the world. This is the foundation upon which change is built.

Next, we must unlearn. We must let go of outdated beliefs, negative thought patterns, and self-limiting notions. Just as a sculptor chips away at a block of marble to reveal the masterpiece within, we must shed the layers that no longer serve us.

Lastly, we must relearn. We must embrace new ways of thinking, forge new neural pathways, and cultivate habits that align with our true selves. This is the process of renewing our minds, as spoken of in Romans 12:2. It requires time, effort, and dedication, but the rewards are immeasurable.

It is time to make a choice. It is time to make new decisions that will shape the course of your life. It is time to create new habits that will guide you towards the life you desire. Embrace the power within you, for the journey ahead holds infinite possibilities.

As we embark on this transformative journey together, let us do so with an inspired heart and an open mind. May the principles we explore become the guiding light that leads us to a life of purpose, joy, and fulfillment.

In Proverbs 4:20–22 MSG, King Solomon says, "Dear friend, listen well to my words; tune your ears to my voice. Keep my message in plain view at all times. Concentrate! Learn it by heart! Those who discover these words live, really live; body and soul, they're bursting with health." Notice that it doesn't say "your mind"; it says, "your heart," something that is wired in. A research done by Dr. J. Andrew Armour who introduced the term, "heart brain," in 1991 discovered that the heart has 40,000 neurons just like the brain. Armour showed that the heart's complex nervous system qualified it as a "little brain." The brain and heart operate independently of each other. Science is now catching up to God's truths because God has been saying it all along.

In the hustle and bustle of our daily lives, it's easy to lose sight of what truly matters. We get caught up in our responsibilities, our to-do lists, and the never-ending demands of the world around us. But amidst the chaos, it's important to carve out moments of stillness and connection with God.

Imagine starting and ending each day with fifteen to thirty precious minutes dedicated solely to your relationship with God. In those first fifteen to thirty minutes, you set the tone for the day ahead. You invite God into your heart, seeking guidance, strength, and wisdom. You surrender your worries and fears, trusting that the Almighty will take care of them. You offer gratitude for the blessings in your life, big and small. And you open yourself up to receive the love and grace that God abundantly pours upon you.

As the day unfolds and you navigate through its twists and turns, you encounter various situations and interactions. Some may uplift you, while others may trigger emotional responses within you. And that's where the last fifteen to thirty minutes of your day come in.

In those precious moments of winding down, you reflect on the events that transpired. You delve into the depths of your emotions, allowing them to rise to the surface. You journal, if that's your practice, capturing the essence of your experiences. You identify the areas that need detoxification, the moments where you may have caused offense or been offended by others. And with the help of the Holy Spirit, your faithful counselor, you seek truth and understanding.

In this process of detoxing, you rewind the day, examining each interaction, conversation, and encounter. You ask yourself, "Where did I offend someone today? Or did someone offend me? And if I was offended, why did it affect me so deeply?" With honesty and humility, you explore the reasons behind your reactions and seek to reset your perspective.

It's important to remember that this new lifestyle of Harpu Practice takes time and practice. You won't master it overnight, but that's okay. What matters is your commitment to growing closer to God, to becoming a better version of yourself each day.

The nighttime detoxing ritual is particularly powerful because it allows you to process the events of the day while they are still fresh. It prevents emotions from festering and helps you release any negativity that may have accumulated. By addressing these issues and seeking the Holy Spirit's guidance, you pave the way for healing and transformation.

So, my friend, I encourage you to embrace this beautiful practice of dedicating the first fifteen minutes and the last fifteen minutes of your day to God. Let His presence infuse your mornings with hope and strength, and let His love cleanse and renew your spirit each night. With patience and perseverance, you will find that this intentional connection with the Divine will transform not only your days but your entire life.

6 Daily Principles to Reset to Original Settings

Day Principles

1. Disrupt: Interrupt your day to start with a mindset of gratitude.
2. Discern: We think, then we feel. Lastly, we choose how to react. We have to catch things before they happen.
3. Destroy: Cast down every negative thought.

Mindfulness is to be practiced all day, and meditation is a time set apart to sink into your heart. Throughout your day, write down your feelings toward people, situations, and circumstances. This can be done mentally or physically on paper or in a note on your phone!

Night Principles

1. Disconnect: Turn everything off and have alone time.
2. Discover: Reconsider your day and read your journals.
3. Detox: Replace the lies with the truth / m.

1. Disrupt

Interrupt your day

When we wake up, we have the highest cortisol level in our body; this is how we are wired. In the past, humans lived in the wild hundreds of years ago, so we could be attacked at any time. We have cortisol in the morning, so we are ready to go into fight or flight mode if a bear is around. But what happens now that there is no bear? God protected us by creating us this way, but who becomes the bear now in modern-day life? The "bear" can take many shapes and sizes in our daily lives. Sometimes, it can be your spouse, children, bills, or the things you lack, and your body doesn't know the difference between your current "bear" and a literal one. So, you are ready to run or fight right when you wake up, even though no real bear is waiting at your bedside. This is why I call the first step disruption because it is not matter over mind; it is mind over matter when we take control.

In the stillness of the morning, as the sun gently rises, we are given a gift. A gift of new beginnings, fresh opportunities, and boundless mercies from above. It is in these moments that we hold the power to transform our very being, to alter the very fabric of our existence.

As we awaken from the depths of slumber, let us not rush to the distractions of the outside world. Instead, let us turn our gaze inward, connecting with the depths of our soul. For it is within ourselves that we find the true essence of who we are, and it is within ourselves that we discover the divine connection that lies dormant, waiting to be awakened.

In this sacred space, we transition from the realms of deep sleep to a state of awareness that I like to call the God zone. It is a state of being in the now, a state of harmony and alignment with the GOD. Some may call it the flow state, where time stands still and we are fully present in the now.

Neuroscience tells us that gratitude has the power to transform. It releases dopamine, the chemical of joy and happiness, while simultaneously reducing cortisol, the stress hormone that plagues our modern lives. This is not a mere coincidence, my friends. It is the profound truth that our thoughts can shape our reality.

Epigenetics, the study of how our environment and experiences influence our genes, affirms this truth. It tells us that thought alone has the power to rewrite the very code of our being. So, let us seize this power, disrupt the patterns of our mornings, and change the chemicals in our bodies. Let us take charge, for we are not mere victims of our biological wiring.

As the morning light bathes us in its gentle glow, let us choose gratitude. Let us choose to be present, to be aware, to be fully alive at this moment. Let us embrace the divine connection within us and allow it to guide us through the day ahead.

In these precious moments of awakening, we are given the opportunity to shape our reality and create a life filled with purpose, joy, and love. So embrace the morning and embrace the power that lies within you. For it is through this power that you can transform not only your own life but the world around you.

Today, and every day, choose to wake up to the beauty within and let it radiate outwards. Embrace the morning, embrace the power of your thoughts, and watch as your life unfolds in ways beyond your wildest dreams.

Gratitude trumps everything

Your morning is the time to disrupt all adverse outcomes by starting with positive thoughts and gratitude and the time to disrupt all negativity. If you have read this far, you are most likely already on your way to transformation. God is doing something in your life, and you are ready to step into all you are destined to be.

Understand that you have the power to change the way you view your circumstances, your surroundings, and the rest of the day. You have the power to change the narrative of the story you believe to be true. This is all dictated by you, and it starts in the morning. Lamentation 3:22- 23 (ESV) teaches that "the steadfast love of the Lord never ceases; his mercies never come to an end; they are new every morning, great is your faithfulness." Take control; this will become a habit after a while, and the world will have to watch out for you!

Now, you can take on your world. Take the first few minutes to thank God that you woke up. Thank him for a new day. This is the moment to establish the day's tone and remind ourselves that we are the creators of our future. It starts in the design of our minds, also known as our landscape. Remember every morning, his mercies are fresh, and we have an opportunity to get it right. Look at it from the beginning of the day if you have a vision. Are you closer to achieving it? What can you do to reach it? What changes can you make?

The morning is critical for setting up a mindful day.

This is so important because I know we can be on the go the minute we wake up at the beginning of the day. However, we must take control and use our first fifteen-thirty minutes to gear up. This is a good starting point, it's the best way to face the challenges of the day. We can focus on what our day should look like rather than have an attitude of que será, será. (a Spanish phrase that means "whatever will be, will be").

Allowing our surroundings to dictate how our days will be is not being in control. Being intentional about our days shows emotional maturity. Taking our days by the horns and deciding to be of value to others allows us to have more control of our day rather than our emotions dictating how we should feel. Recite scripture, and start your day with God. Later I will share with you scriptures that have helped me on this journey. Write down how you want your day to begin. This activity keeps you engaged during the day so that you are intentionally setting goals. There are places you need to be, and things you need to achieve.

I'll give you a secret that helped me early on my walks. I meditate on God's love. This spiritual truth has gotten me so far, and everything opposite of this truth wasn't the place I wanted to be.

If I felt anxiety, I would automatically know this was not of God. I would tell myself, "This is not peace!" I would then adjust my thoughts quickly, for I knew I was most likely making a future problem a reality when, in fact, it wasn't a problem. We have the power to change the narrative of any circumstance in our lives. This would be my declaration early in the morning. This statement would filter what happened during the day. If it prevented me from acting this way, I would automatically discern and react to adjust my attitude. This has been so effective in my life and still is. The mental warfare is real and this is how we fight it.

2. Discern Your Thoughts and Heart

Discerning Thoughts

Dr. Caroline Leaf stated, "We are thinking, feeling, choosing beings." We can choose to make a difference from now on. I can change my outcome by taking control of my thought life now. This principle here is a lifelong one, and once you get good at discernment, you're on your way to freedom. Oxford languages define "discernment" as follows

1. The ability to judge well.
2. Perception in the absence of judgment to obtain spiritual guidance and understanding.

Discernment happens in our frontal lobe daily. This is where we judge every thought. No one ever told me this, so I would just let every thought in, and I'm sure you might as well. This reminds me of a movie where a parent went away and told their kids that no one could come over. The kids agreed, only to cave into their friends' ideas and throw a party that everyone was invited to. No one watched the door to see whom they let in, and little did they know they were hosting the wrong crowd. These guests later would trash the house and leave everything destroyed. When we let every thought in carelessly, we cannot discern who is at the door. We then start to host every thought that comes in; many to destroy us.

Anxiety, depression, bitterness, and low self-esteem can be products of our thinking. However, we must remember that we think, feel, and choose. We get to choose what we believe in and give our energy to. We become the parents of these thoughts by giving them our focus. We fuel them, and these very thoughts are the ones that take us from homeostasis (calm) to fight-or-flight mode (chaos).

Neuroscience states that we activate hormones and chemicals by thoughts alone. Every time we are angry, we release fourteen hundred toxins and thirty hormones, which rush through our bodies like flushes of heat, and six minutes of anger later, this shuts down our immune system for twenty-one hours. This is what we do to ourselves by not discerning our thoughts. When we actively discern our thoughts, we can realize whether these thoughts are for us or against us. We can then choose to abort negative thoughts immediately.

This happens before our eyes—or, more correctly, between our eyes. We have sixty thousand thoughts a day, and out of the sixty thousand thoughts, 91 percent are reoccurring. Now that you know this, you can choose what to spend your day thinking about. Like a muscle, the more you practice controlling your mind, the better you get at it. We can take thoughts captive like prisoners and interrogate them to see where they come from. We must ask the Holy Spirit and discern; if a thought is unfavorable, we must cast it down! We will be saving space in our thoughts. Thoughts allow us to restructure our inner landscape to create our desired life. So what are you thinking about? Is it producing life or death? Don't parent thoughts that later grow up and make a mess in your house. As we learn to discipline our thought lives, you will enjoy your journey.

"See, I set before you today life and prosperity, death and destruction" (Deuteronomy 30:15 NIV). The principle of choices will sum up our lives from now on. We don't have to be enslaved by our old thinking and allow in any thought that knocks at our door. We learn these principles early in life but never use them in our thinking process. But think about it, we shouldn't open the door to any thought.

Discerning the Heart

Matthew 7:20 (ESV) states, "Thus you will recognize them by their fruits." The fruits Jesus describes here are the by-products of our intentions and, most importantly, our hearts. If we ever truly desire to live peaceful, joyous, and happy lives, we must become inspectors of our hearts. What provokes negative emotions within you? When do these emotions occur? Around whom?

This principle is about discerning what is destroying us from within our hearts. Recently, I read a story about a fish kill. This is a phenomenon that happens in the environment that causes masses of fish to die. After carefully investigating this case, institutions came to understand the problem. There was a shortage of algae, which produces oxygen, in the water. When the environment doesn't sustain the algae, the fish die. I never knew that fish could suffocate, but what happens is that a lack of oxygen usually produced by the algae causes the fish to die.

So, it is within us. The algae represent God's love, and when this love is not present, it takes the oxygen away from our lives. I'm not talking about the external environment; I'm talking about the internal environment of our hearts. If you're still living with the conditions of the past, this is not giving you the breath of life. Something is missing to sustain your mortal life, and we find ourselves dying internally from a lack of oxygen in our souls.

I mentioned earlier that metacognition allows us to know what we're thinking about. And being able to discern this will allow us to know what is adversely affecting us by jarring us out of peace. Have you ever noticed how you can be at peace but then see a person (we all have someone that pushes our buttons, causing us to go into a warlike mode), and then you're ready for war? You are in a fight-or-flight situation, and we usually choose to fight. We want to work on this to make a life that's buttonless. No one should be able to take you out of your peace by pressing buttons in your heart. Once you achieve this, you will encounter a special peace. "And the peace of God, which surpasses all understanding, will guard your hearts and minds in Christ Jesus" (Philippians 4:7 ESV).

The ancient prophet Jeremiah also warns about our heart when he states, "The heart is deceitful above all things and desperately sick; who can understand it?" (Jeremiah 17:9 ESV). We might not fully understand it, but we can discern it. Sometimes, we don't even have to see people, but only in our minds remember what they did. Remember the brain doesn't know the difference. The virtual reality glasses of your mind perceive it as present, and your heart alerts you with the warlike mode of the fight-or-flight response. This is what we want to disarm the enemy of. You can sense something, but it doesn't have to dictate the rest of your day. No one should have this kind of authority over us. No one should dictate how we feel. Only God should have this ability!

Remember our hearts are like check engine lights. When it flashes in your car, you don't ignore it. It's the same with us and our hearts. Sometimes, our hearts come out of peace, and the pressure breaks us down. We say all is well when, in reality, it is not. Something is wrong with the engine (heart), but we don't want to look deep to find the problem. Our check engine light is flashing, and we keep driving. The flashing check engine light is our state of mind. It is a statement from the heart warning us that something is wrong. Just like a check engine light tells us that something needs to be addressed, this could happen with our situation. Yet, we keep ignoring the check engine light. We must open the hood and do the work to see change.

The ancient King Solomon of Israel wrote, "Above all else, watch over your heart; diligently guard it because the good and noble things of life come from a sincere and pure heart" (Proverbs 4:23 VOICE)

Write down these instances where you have been removed from your inner peace. Remember, you must go inside the engine and replace some parts. I want you to know that this is not a sprint; this is a journey, and these principles will allow you to navigate to your correct destination—the destination God intended for you, not the one that the enemy designed for you. The enemy aims to steal, kill, and destroy. That is his objective. The opposing forces never want you to achieve anything positive. Thankfully, as we do the work of discerning the heart, we will know life and life more abundantly in Christ (John 10:10 NKJV).

3. Destroy

"Casting down arguments, and every high thing that exalts itself against the knowledge of God and bringing into captivity every thought" (2 Corinthians 10:5 ESV). The ability to dictate what you invest your energy in is vitally important. We can be so careless with our thought lives that we allow any thought and give it life by giving it our full attention. That is how we birth negative thoughts. Negativity takes away or withdraws quality from your life. The question is, what does it subtract from our lives?

Negative thoughts subtract from the fruits of the spirit detailed in Galatians. Negative thoughts detract from your love, joy, peace, patience, kindness, goodness, gentleness, faithfulness, and self-control. The good news is that you can cast them down, reject them, and opt not to give them energy or life by meditating on them. Why not? Because once we allow them into our lives, they take away, withdraw, and steal. The purpose of negative thoughts is to steal, kill, and destroy what God has for us. But we have the power to cast them down and not let them in. To attain inner freedom, you must be able to objectively watch your problems instead of being lost in them.

We can choose to be the main actors in our lives or the costars. We choose. "Getting your thoughts disciplined and under control is one of the first steps in freeing yourself of the world's burdens and beginning to enjoy life despite the burdens of the world."

The apostle Paul warns that we should not give the devil a "foothold in our lives" (Ephesians 4:27 NIV). We give thoughts our energy by allowing negative thinking to nurture within our minds and feed them with our attention. The purpose of these negative thoughts is to reach your heart, but they enter your mind first. Then, as you continue to rehearse your thoughts over and over whichever one you value most, gets sorted at night from short-term memory to long-term memory; what I call the heart, this is the hippocampus's job. It's the enemy trying to work from within because he wants to work from your heart, not your mind. We must decide not to allow that to continue happening in our lives. We must take control of our thoughts by pulling the reins on our emotions and not allowing just any thought to linger.

We must take control of our minds and what we spend our energy on. What we focus on is giving life and growth. Remember where your focus goes, energy follows. A spiritual principle from the apostle Paul says, "Finally, brethren, whatsoever things are true, whatsoever things are honest, whatsoever things are just, whatsoever things are pure, whatsoever things are lovely, whatsoever things are of good report; if there be any virtue, and if there be any praise, think on these things." (Philippians 4:8 KJV).

If you're going to think about anything, think about good things. Think about the Word of God that testifies. It is life for those who receive it. Think about where God is taking you. Think of what's true. Think of the things that are honest and just, pure and lovely—anything of good report. Spend your energy on these things. Take control of your thought life; once you master this area, you will never be the same. You'll be elevated to new levels of joy!

Another key spiritual principle is "For as he thinketh in his heart, so is he" (Proverbs 23:7 KJV). If our thinking produces a reality in our lives and some of our thoughts are negative, our existence will be negative. Imagine if you take control of your thought life and are always in line with the Word of God. Imagine your destination if you shift your thinking habits around, stop meditating on the wrong things that drain you, and start meditating on the right things thoughts that will build us up and encourage us to inspire those around us. This is a new way of life once you embrace this and know the direction of your life depends on how well you judge your thoughts.

Our ability to discern our thoughts and cast down negative thoughts enables us to be edified. Our meditation on those things that build us up and do not tear us down will continually create an atmosphere of growth. Remember we are thinking, feeling, and choosing beings. If we control the first part of our thinking, we control our feelings and choices. With this, we can choose life instead of death, joy instead of sorrow, peace instead of chaos, and the best instead of the worst. This is what happens when we take hold of our thought lives. What directs our destiny today changes the day we take control, and we will release the power to create what God intended for us to have!

Dr. Caroline Leaf, in Switch on Your Brain, says, "When we direct our rest by introspection, self-reflection, and prayer; when we catch our thoughts; when we memorize and quote Scripture; and when we develop our mind intellectually, we enhance the default mode network (DMN) that improves brain function and mental, physical, and spiritual health." As we think about what we think, we can default back to God's original image described in Genesis 1:26–28 NIV.

What we think about becomes who we are and if this is, in fact, the case, then should we decide today what we will think about in advance?

Mindful Journaling

"See to it that no one falls short of God's grace; that no root of resentment springs up and causes trouble" (Hebrews 12:15 NKJV). Again, I want to stress writing down what your heart is feeling toward people, situations, and circumstances. This is a simple practice, but it is essential because it keeps us accountable for working on the issues of the heart. Whatever moves your attitude toward stress or anger throughout the day, please write it down. If your heart alerts you that something is wrong, write it down. If someone triggers something, write it down. If you find yourself sweating at the mere presence of someone, write it down. Don't be alarmed at how much you write; just write!

This is a marathon, not a sprint. We will work at it little by little. Make an oath to take the future by the reins and start working on creating your intended destiny. These daily starting principles are essential. It's also good that you start journaling it all. What you have journaled will always be something you can always go back to and measure your progress against. What bothers you today won't be doing that for long because you have chosen to do something about it.

This principle of mindfulness is intended to be an exercise of self-awareness and self-improvement all in one. While you journal, you will discover patterns that have changed and those that need changing. All will become clearer to you as the days move along. Don't allow yourself to depend on your memory in this drawing phase. Our memories will always have us believe what we want to believe, and this won't always be based on factual events. If you write it as it happens, you will be better suited to drawing a picture of the real you.

The Nighttime Practices

We can follow the nighttime practices, including disconnecting from our day, entering a meditative state, discovering our inner self, and allowing the Holy Spirit to renew our minds.

For the first fifteen to thirty minutes of your nighttime routine, you want to start with disconnecting and being mindful. Disconnection means to separate something from something else or create a connection between two or more things. It is the ability to let everything go. When the day is almost over, set aside some alone time and remind yourself that you deserve this moment. You have worked hard all day, and this is the time when you get to relax. To have the body, soul, and spirit be at peace, we must provide ourselves with this disconnecting moment. Hebrews 4:1 (TPT) states, "Now God has offered us the promise of entering into his realm of resting in confident faith. So, we must be cautious to ensure that we all embrace the fullness of that promise and not fail to experience it." We must strive to find our way back into this rest.

Homeostasis occurs when the body, soul, and spirit are in line, in perfect harmony and peace. It's when we are one with God in Harpu. We can arrive at this place by preparing ourselves for inner engineering where we can change programs in our hearts.

4. Disconnect (Mindfulness)

Let's start by disconnecting. Spend the first five to ten minutes in this step. The art of mindfulness is being present now. The ability to disconnect from the outer world and align yourself with your inner world.

We can always increase the time we set aside, but for the sake of starting small and adding a new routine, let's keep it small. Allow yourself to go from this world of chaos and enter peace. Instead of watching that drama on TV before you sleep, be mindful and disconnect. We have enough drama in our lives; we do not need to spend the last moments of our day in other people's drama. This is what we want to change and have less drama, less chaos, and fewer battles.

We can't afford any influences from the outside. Did you know that the subconscious, the symbolic heart, does not stop working? Even when you fall asleep, it's in charge of the many functions of your body. Imagine if the subconscious went to sleep. Many of the functions of our bodies would cease. Then what would we have? A very long sleep. We might meet the Creator! Just kidding! That won't happen. The subconscious never sleeps, and anything we see right before we go to sleep can influence an attitude in our hearts.

Anything chaotic that you watch, see, or hear before sleep produces an influence in your subconscious (heart). Then, we wonder why we wake up with argumentative attitudes. We refer to waking up on the wrong side of the bed as waking up on the same side after having outside influences working on us while we sleep. It puts us on the wrong side of the bed, moving us from calm into chaos. "Be angry and do not sin; do not let the sun go down on your anger" (Ephesians 4:26 ESV).

Let's create an atmosphere of peace before we go to sleep that produces life in us! This is our moment to let go of the day's worries, problems, situations with the kids, and bills. This is our moment to put everything aside and remember that we'll go to sleep after this moment. Let's create an atmosphere of well-being for our hearts to rest while we sleep and for the Word of Truth to penetrate our hearts and create a new self. To return to the original settings, you must be the inner engineer, align everything correctly, and set it back to its original settings through God's truth.

For this to happen, we must be at peace and allow ourselves to go into our subconscious to program (renew our minds and hearts) and align with God's spiritual truths about ourselves. We must change some of our philosophies, ideologies, and beliefs that have been programmed early in our lives that are not truths. We have attained them through words, environment, culture, and family as early as our third trimester in our mother's womb as mentioned before. These concepts don't align with the spiritual truths about us or God's intent in our lives. They are attained through emotions, fears, and words that don't connect with our destinies but are lies. They are hollow and deceptive and produce no fruits in our lives.

I promise you that the time you spend with yourself, taking charge of your future, and the power and authority you have to re-engineer your heart and take the future by the reins will all be worth it.

We can remove what needs to be removed from our hearts and replace it with life-giving words. Take this moment to be mindful of the ability to go from beta brain waves to alpha brain waves. This brings us to mind and heart coherence. It is a disconnection from reality into spirituality and takes us from a place of limits to a place of limitlessness. It is a moment when we can create and imagine where we want to go. It's a moment when we forget about everything (time, place) just to be in homeostasis with the one true God. Here, we become one with him in mindfulness in Harpu. This is art! This will allow you to disconnect from reality and enter the supernatural realm.

This is a space where we can escape the chatterbox of this world and just sit still and hear from God. Even though I have allocated only five to ten minutes for this step, you can expand this time as you get better at silencing the chatterbox of life. Because it is crucial, you can spend thirty, forty-five, or even an hour on this step. As you unwind, you're activating genes to shift the inside of your body to accommodate a moment of peace and bring your whole body into perfect harmony. You will be taking away the effects of stress and the hormones associated with stress to get your body back into a place of peace where it can fix and restore itself to do what it's supposed to do by nature. Your body will reorganize and heal itself. All these things are only a byproduct of taking your body, soul, and spirit into a place of homeostasis. This is the place of our original settings where we can function correctly.

These first minutes are the key to the next step because it makes self-discovery hard if you don't reach that place of peace. When I say "self-discovery," it refers to self-awareness of the imperfections programmed within our subconscious that were found and written down. In this next step, you will be going over what you journal about yourself during the day. What have you noticed outside of the program? This is called multiple-perspective advantage (MPA), coined by neuroscientist Dr. Caroline Leaf. We are the only species that can step outside our thoughts and inspect them, or as I mentioned earlier in the book metacognition. We must learn this to see and understand where we need inner engineering. In this next state, we can only start fixing something when we know it is broken.

We can't find answers if we look into this area of our lives with materialistic lenses—the carnal mind rather than the spiritual mind. But if we look at the physical part of who we are through our spiritual lenses in mindfulness, we can devise a plan to adjust certain things in our lives and replace some lies with truths.

I want you to be aware of these things. We are made up of 7 octillion atoms which, according to science, are made of 0.00000000000001 percent particle material and 99.99999999999 percent spirit energy. Yet, we want to discover more of the particle material than spiritual energy. The more significant amount of who we are lies in the understanding that we are two-thirds spiritual and one-third particle material. We are more spiritual than particles; in order to change the particle we must change the spiritual. If we can grab hold of this truth and connect with all we are, we will be unstoppable. Can you imagine the possibilities that we can have access to? We can connect with God and for him to intervene and start creating and changing our hearts. Then, we can navigate and end up where he originally intended to go. Our purpose is the destination! Imagine the possibilities of going beyond what we see and venturing deeper into who we are. This step will take time and persistence to master, but once you do, you're well on your way to a new self.

5. Discover (Know thyself)

We love vacations because we like to discover new things. We are so curious about discovering that we made it to the moon. However, we haven't scratched the surface of our hearts. We don't want to discover ourselves internally and know what makes us who we are, so we continually look for things to keep us busy. We don't want to deal with ourselves. We would instead focus on what's outside.

I remember watching a show called Hoarders. It was about people who kept so many things in their houses that it became impossible for them to live there. This occurred because they did not want to let go of anything they had acquired over the years. In the show, counselors would go into their homes. The counselors would say, "Hey, we get that it is hard, but we must clean this up because you can't stay here any longer. You don't even have space to live here. You must move out of your house because you would rather keep old newspapers and furniture than toss them out and make space for you to live."

So, it is in the spiritual realm. We become spiritual hoarders when we can't process negative emotions that get stored in our bodies. A great way to explain this is that the body keeps score of the negative input. This prevents us from being in a place of peace and living in the now. It is overwhelming, and this is when we begin to look for peace from external enjoyment, pleasure, and distractions. A constant lifestyle of this mindset creates an area of depression. Studies have shown that an unbalance of hormones and brain chemistry contributes to this state of being. We don't want to get there. However, to grow, we must go into the house and start taking out things that take up space.

As we take this journey, remember that if we don't know the core of the problem, we can't resolve it. How can we say we are free when we are in bondage to our past emotions? This journey is to release some of the prisoners you have kept deep inside your heart where no one can see them. In this discovery step, we create new experiences, acquire a new mindset, and create new narratives to shift our future. We are finding some of the hurts from our past to set us free. We will not hold any prisoner in our hearts; if we do, the real prisoner is ourselves. Like in the movie "The Secret in Their Eyes," starring Nicole Kidman and Julia Roberts, we will wear away when we hold on to an offense. The prison door of unforgiveness can be opened only from the inside, for when we place someone in that cell, we go inside with them, and only we hold the key. This is a great movie to watch to see the effects of someone who holds onto negative emotions that are stored in the heart.

We must make space for new things—the new version of ourselves. Please think of this: whenever we have too much on our plates from our pasts, we run out of space to create the future. I remember taking my first iPhone to the shop because it was malfunctioning. It was running slowly, and every app felt like it was glitching. My phone would cut out, and it became increasingly annoying. I went to the Apple Store (the store of the device's manufacturer) with the idea that if anyone knew what was wrong with my device, it would be the one who created it. I told the Apple guy, "It's not working right!" They looked at it, made a diagnosis, and concluded that I had too much information on it—too many pictures and videos. I also had thirty apps open!

I take pictures of everything, and this picture-taking was costing me delays on my phone. I had too many photos and videos of the past. My phone couldn't handle the pressure of all the open apps, pictures, and videos. The guy told me I had to delete some photos and videos for my phone to work correctly. I also had to close every application. Doing this would allow the phone to work correctly. While he said this, I thought, isn't this the way we are in the spiritual world? We're not running right because we have too many pictures and videos of the past! Open apps are like open issues that were never dealt with—unprocessed emotions. Having too many suppressed problems prevents us from functioning as we should. It takes up all our space, and we have no room in our hearts to become all God intended us to be!

Upon reflection, it is essential for us to take a step back and examine our inner workings. This brings us to the principle, which emphasizes the importance of introspection. By detaching ourselves from our usual thought patterns and venturing into the realm of metacognition, we gain the ability to observe our subconscious minds and unravel the intricacies that drive us.

In this process of self-analysis, we have the opportunity to identify the beliefs and programming that shape our thoughts and actions. By delving deeper into our hearts, we can discern which aspects need to be realigned with spiritual truths. This act of introspection enables us to become aware of the origins of our thoughts, allowing us to discern whether they are rooted in our own authentic selves or have been influenced by external factors.

Metacognition, this gift of self-awareness, empowers us to rise above our ordinary thinking patterns. Through its lens, we can critically examine our thoughts and motivations, shedding light on the subconscious programs that guide our behavior. By doing so, we uncover the hidden layers of our programming, enabling us to recognize where adjustments and reprogramming are necessary to align ourselves with spiritual truths.

In the midst of chaos and uncertainty, take a moment to reflect on moments throughout the day. To remember what occurred, journaling is the best way to go back to review what happened. It may seem like a simple act, but it holds the key to unlocking your true potential. As you flip through the pages of your journal, you'll discover a treasure trove of emotions, thoughts, and experiences that make up the tapestry of your life.

This journey of self-discovery is not a race, my friend. It's a marathon that requires patience, perseverance, and a deep understanding of yourself. Embrace the process, for it is in the stillness of reflection that we can truly grow.

With each stroke of your pen during the day, you reveal a piece of your soul. You unearth dreams, desires, fears, and aspirations that may have been buried beneath the weight of daily life. Your journal becomes a safe haven, a sanctuary where you can pour out your heart and explore the depths of your being.

In this moment, as you review the words you have penned throughout the day, remember that change takes time. Rome wasn't built in a day, and neither will your transformation be. But trust in the process, for every small step forward brings you closer to the person you long to become.

Take this time to assess what needs to change in your life. Are there habits, relationships, or mindsets that no longer serve you? Recognize that you have the power to shape your own destiny. By changing yourself, you create a ripple effect that can transform your entire environment and generation.

Believe in your ability to make a difference, my friend. Your journal holds the key to unlocking your potential, and it is through self-reflection that you will find the answers you seek. Embrace this moment of the night as an opportunity to work towards the changes you desire.

As you embark on this journey in the evening of self-discovery, remember that you are not alone. You have the support of your journal, your thoughts, and the Holy Spirit. Trust yourself, and know that you are capable of achieving greatness. Explore the depths of your soul, uncover hidden truths, and set your intentions for a brighter future. This is your moment, your time to shine.

When I started doing this, I started noticing many character flaws deep inside of me that I was not aware of. But once I became more aware, the flaws lost its power. I started tackling these character defects. I started searching for the deeper roots that made me the way I am. These things were deep in my heart. This is why Jeremiah, the Old Testament prophet, said, "The heart is deceitful above all things and desperately sick; who can understand it?" (Jeremiah 17:9 ESV).

If we want to change, we have to see ourselves from the perspective of the outside (metacognition) as I stated earlier. Many of our character flaws are deeply rooted in bitterness, anger, resentment, and unforgiveness for things that happened in the past. These are the areas where we must apply forgiveness at the root so that they stop manifesting in our lives. Jesus said you would recognize them by their fruits (Luke 6:44). The main objective here is the roots. The fruits are the symptoms of the problem, and recognizing the origins of our behavior is the big win. We can tackle only what we notice at the root. I challenge you to step out of the shadows and see yourself as you are. Only then can you truly move toward the light of all you are destined to be.

I remember one time when I was on a treadmill, and the small voice inside my heart whispered, "The world is in dire need of vitamin L." As I started pondering on this, my mind went to a previous moment when I went to the doctor for a backache, fatigue, and muscle aches. Then they did bloodwork, which revealed a deficiency in vitamin D. The doctor told me I needed more vitamin D and prescribed a supplement. He did not deal with my symptoms one by one. He went to the root of the problem, a deficiency in an area of my life. So it is with us. Our sinful actions and wrong choices are symptoms; they are not the core problem.

Humanity has a deficiency in vitamin L (vitamin love). People are lacking in love. When we are deficient in God's kind of love in our lives, we see it manifesting in our lives in the form of the following symptoms:

- wrong choices
- anger
- bitterness
- depression
- anxiety
- adultery
- murder

These are all symptoms of the heart, but we shouldn't deal with the problems individually. We must attack the root, and the way to do this is by applying the solution: love.Grace.Forgiveness, The more we know that God loves us, the fewer symptoms will come out of our lives. We are loved because forgiveness has taken place through Jesus. When we receive this love, we can arm ourselves with the same forgiveness and apply it in our lives for others. We can forgive when we understand that he died for us so that we can give that same forgiveness to others forgiveness is for giving not for keeping. "Our love for others is our grateful response to the love God first demonstrated to us" (1 John 3:19 TPT).

Freedom can be achieved, but we must let go of the past to achieve it. When we don't let go, we live there and repeatedly feel the emotions. This destroys us internally. To enjoy God's presence, we must enhance this present day.

Behavior modification only cuts out the fruit, but sooner or later, we know that the fruits of character flaws eventually come out again in a different season. To go into a deeper state of change, we must go into these areas of our lives with forgiveness in both hands: one to apply forgiveness to self, and the other to apply forgiveness to the person who is the root of the problem. Whatever may have started in our childhood must be confronted. Usually, our childhood is where we have the origins of anger, resentment, bitterness, and hatred when it should have been love, grace, and forgiveness. It begins with our immediate family and stems out to the world early on in life. We must go to the root (the person) and apply forgiveness to change in this area. Forgiveness is not a feeling, it is a choice.

It takes too much effort to hold on to unforgiveness because having unforgiveness drains our energy, life source, and space where God should be. To keep these accounts open is to keep them alive in our subconscious. When they are open in our hearts, they steal, kill and destroy, even influence our personalities. These are negative things in our lives. The word "negative" means "something that takes away." As long as we keep these things in our hearts, they will keep draining our lives away and taking up space. We become spiritual hoarders. God, every morning, provides a new day of life, and all these toxic emotions toward people take the bulk of your life resources to keep them alive. These negative emotions take up our creative life source and destroy us from within.

Here's an example. Some lamps have variable brightness. In other words, every time we touch them, they get brighter. However, the opposite is also true. Once they reach the highest brightness, they grow dimmer whenever you touch them. This happens when we have unforgiveness, resentment, and bitterness in our hearts. It's as if we are at the highest level when we wake up, but all these past areas touch our life sources and dim us down, and this is how we continue our day. Please understand this: when you have unforgiveness, bitterness, anger, and resentment toward anyone in your life, you are feeding it by keeping the account of the offense as a debt that still needs to be paid.

We must come to an understanding that the mercies of God are fresh every morning. He covers us with his grace, and we need to take this grace and forgiveness and have so much of it in the morning that we disperse it during the day, especially in the areas of our past. If you want to grow and achieve everything God has for you, use these moments of discovery. You must allow God to show you the areas that you need to apply forgiveness to so that these areas of your life are no longer draining you with the help of the Holy Spirit (the counsel). This is the most significant way to release yourself from the bondage of the past. The chains holding you back are broken when you set those who hurt and betrayed you free by canceling that debt. This is not something you have to do by yourself, it is with the Holy Spirit.

In the depths of your soul, there lies a power that is beyond comprehension. It is the power of love, a love that knows no boundaries, no limits, and no conditions. It is the love that God pours into your being every single day. When you grasp the magnitude of this love, something incredible happens. You become aware of the immense worth and value that you possess. You realize that you are cherished, cherished by the creator of the universe. How can you not feel empowered by such a realization?

With this newfound awareness, a remarkable transformation takes place within you. Suddenly, the hurt inflicted upon you by others loses its sting. You no longer hold onto resentment or anger. Instead, you choose to love those who have hurt you. And here's the beautiful truth: you have the ability to love them not with your own limited human love, but with the boundless love of God. It is a love that surpasses understanding, a love that goes beyond what is expected.

Loving your enemies may seem like an impossible task, but it is in this act of love that you discover true liberation. You break free from the chains of bitterness and resentment that hold you captive. You rise above the darkness and step into the light. In the face of adversity, let love be your guiding force. Let it be the compass that directs your actions and words. Let it be the armor that protects your heart from turning cold and callous. Remember, each day is a new opportunity to receive God's love, and to be filled to the brim with His grace. Embrace this love and let it flow through you, touching the lives of those around you. The steadfast love of the Lord never ceases; His mercies never come to an end; They are new every morning; Great is your faithfulness. (Lamentations 3:22–23 ESV)

This means we have access to this love to apply it to those areas and people who hurt us so that they do not become burdens in our lives. Perhaps they forgot they hurt you, but it's okay. You have held them captive inside your heart long enough.

Have you become an accountant in the spiritual realm? You have been feeding them, nurturing them, because there is a debt that must be paid in your mind and that is the narrative you tell yourself. They owe you, and they are going to pay one day for what they did to you. Does this sound like the narrative you hear in your head? You have a tight bookkeeping system on offenses yet have forgotten that the debt God paid for our transgressions was covered and erased as though it never happened. But, little old, you are holding on to one bitterness? The real prisoner here is you!

The most significant part of this journey is understanding how much God loves us so that we can apply this love (agape or unconditional love) to those who seemingly do not deserve it. Unconditional love is love with no conditions. To receive it, we do nothing. We don't deserve this love, yet he lavishes us with it. God's unconditional love is not based on our performance. We receive it solely based on his love for us. Whom do we think we are putting a condition on whom we should love? Once we are awakened to this truth, we will be free to live the way God wants us to.

Another principle Jesus spoke about is how knowing the truth will set you free. The word "know" here is translated from the Greek word "Kinosko." "Kinosko" means "To become one with truth in the heart." The most significant truth we have in our hearts is that we are loved by God unconditionally, with no strings attached. With this truth, we can go forward and love the unlovable, empowered with agape love. Once this area of self-reflecting and discovering clicks, it becomes the greatest part of this journey.

Train yourself to mentally think life-giving thoughts and push play or fast-forward more than you press rewind when thinking about your life. Close the apps. Delete the old pictures and videos. Close all open doors and windows of unforgiveness. Do the hard work of discovery to lead you to the final step of detoxing your day.

6. Detox

Detox is "a process or period in which one abstains from or rids the body of toxic or unhealthy substances." In this principle, it will take some time to eliminate the toxicity in your thought life and heart realm. In the previous principle, discovery, we hopefully found some areas we needed to work on. But in this step, we start applying the changes discovered.

We already know that out of the sixty thousand thoughts we have daily, 90 percent are recurrent thoughts stemming from the heart and 70 percent are negative. This is the step we want to use to eliminate toxicity from our negative emotions and views from the past. We want to create new thoughts, feelings, and experiences and establish new life directions. We want to experience God's promise of newness, which is described in the Old Testament by the ancient prophet Isaiah, "Stop dwelling on the past. Don't even remember these former things. I am doing something brand-new, something unheard of. Even now, it sprouts and grows and matures. Don't you perceive it? I will make a way in the wilderness and open up flowing streams in the desert. (Isaiah 43:18–19 TPT)

We begin by removing from the old thought patterns the sting of pain attached to them. The way we do this is to apply forgiveness to the person attached to the events, and in doing so, we remove the sting of pain attached to it. You will never forget the event, but no negative emotion will be attached to it. You will have defeated the enemy, although sometimes the enemy is us. I've noticed sometimes that we have to repeat this step a few times. But as you continue to bring awareness to those areas in your life, change the narrative, and apply forgiveness. You will continue to get to the original setting, one victory at a time, one event at a time, one moment at a time, one trauma at a time. Freedom begins to peak as you continue to win every battle.

We develop the ability to adjust some gauges inside our hearts that produce original settings that operate in our outer lives. This part of your detoxification begins in the spiritual realm first but manifests itself in the physical outer realm. We must start looking at negative emotions as stealing life from us daily. We must stop allowing our past to determine what grows in the gardens of our minds.

We must take back our lives. Dr. Kim D'eramo shared a study on people's minds and energy fields. Energy fields are enlarged with love and shrink with negative thoughts. Science keeps pointing to the truths about God and his principles by making this the most significant moment to combine both. The coming together of science and spirituality is helping to bring us to a place where we can be at peace in homeostasis with the one true God who loves us unconditionally and wants the best for us. If you're a parent, you know that no parent wants the worst for their kids. Parents want the best at all times. Imagine God, who created us. He wants the best for us; we have everything we need to accomplish this. It's time we stop giving away our creative nature to past hurts and future problems that might never happen.

We take our authority and apply forgiveness to remove the sting of pain. When we choose to forgive, this shifts and changes the landscapes of our minds. Harvard studies suggest that forgiveness is associated with lower levels of depression, anxiety, and hostility. The opposite of this must be true: if we suffer these symptoms, we could still have unforgiveness in our hearts.

During this time ask the Holy Spirit to reveal the truth about people in your life. This is the detox state, the most crucial practice to end the night. Make space by choosing to forgive. Remember: forgiveness is not a feeling but a choice; we forgive because we want to make space for God. At this moment, think of whoever is coming to your heart from your discovery that you need to forgive. Confess with your mouth the following prayer:

I choose to forgive _____ for _____. This debt is canceled! They owe me nothing. Just as Jesus forgave all my sins from my past, my present, and my future. I also choose to forgive in the same manner.

Congratulations on taking the first step towards change! This is a momentous occasion, as it marks the beginning of a new chapter in your life. It takes courage and determination to embark on a journey of self-improvement, and you should be incredibly proud of yourself for making this commitment. You have recognized the need for change and have chosen to embrace it wholeheartedly. This shows incredible strength and resilience. Remember, change is not always easy, but it is always worth it. It is through change that we grow, learn, and become the best versions of ourselves. As you embark on this journey, keep in mind that the path ahead may be filled with obstacles and challenges. But don't let that discourage you. Remember that every obstacle is an opportunity for growth and every challenge is a chance to prove your strength.

CHAPTER 12

PROGRAMMING YOUR HEART

My heartfelt desire is for you to receive newness in all areas of your life. I pray that a passion for new ways of thinking will lead you to new ways of living. As you dive into this chapter, you will find some fundamental practices to apply to your life that will be beneficial in living the life you've always desired.

I have studied the Jewish culture because Jesus is a descendant of this lineage. I have learned a critical component from the Jewish tradition which they established from youth for their generational success which is meditating on His Word day and night. This allows them to plant the Word of God in their hearts as written in Psalm 1:2–3 (NKJV):

But his delight is in the law of the Lord,
And in His law, he [a]meditates day and night.
He shall be like a tree
Planted by the [b]rivers of water,
That brings forth its fruit in its season,
Whose leaf also shall not wither;
And whatever he does shall prosper.

In my studies, I have learned that in a Jewish household, by the age of five, they are studying Mikra, at ten studying Mishnah, and at thirteen fulfilling the mitzvot which consists of studying and memorizing scripture.

By the age of thirteen, before the Bar Mitzvah ("coming of age"), they must publicly recite certain scriptures, to commemorate the young boys and girls into adulthood. Another recitation of scripture is done by placing a mezuzah, a historical symbol, in a place where they can see it every day. The mezuzah is placed in the doorpost of the home as a constant reminder of God's dwelling and blessing in our lives. One thing I have noticed is that in my walk with Christ, I wasn't intentional about having scriptures etched in my heart to meditate day and night to remind me of the goodness of God. What would it look like if we were daily reminded of His love, our identity in His love, our freedom, authority, and our eternal promises? Could this be the way to victory in overcoming the daily obstacles in our minds—by reciting His Word? Could it be that we have the Ark of the Covenant in our hearts and it is up to us to place the scroll of his word in our innermost being? In this chapter, I will discuss the twelve scriptural pillars of life that have guided me and transformed me.

I first heard of Scud missiles when reading about the Iraq War. The purpose of this weapon is to deflect incoming missiles in the air, preventing them from damaging land targets. So these twelve verses will be like Scud missiles planted in your heart so that when the enemy sends a missile or fiery dart into your thought life, it will be diverted so it never reaches your heart. So, let's get ready to change the battlefield.

Twenty-One Days Create a New Habit; Ninety Days Creates a New Life

Before walking into a new life, we must create new habits. This is vitally important for us to understand. Winston Churchill, in 1906 stated: "Where there is great power, there is great responsibility..."

To walk in the fullness of God's promises, we will begin creating the habits needed to sustain this new life. Let us read the apostle Paul's encouragement as we develop new habits. "And he has taught you to let go of the lifestyle of the ancient man, the old self-life, which was corrupted by sinful and deceitful desires that spring from delusions. Now it's time to be made new by every revelation given to you. And to be transformed as you embrace the glorious Christ-within as your new life and live in union with him! For God has recreated you in his perfect righteousness, and you now belong to him in the realm of true holiness" (Ephesians 4:22–24 TPT).

Makings of change

All change begins with us first knowing that changes are needed. However, change cannot be wished into existence. Change becomes change when we decide to change. We will be exploring together the key ingredients that have helped me change. They are my secrets. When added to your daily prayer it takes you to the next level.

In this chapter, we will explore twelve scriptural pillars that will serve as a guard for our hearts. We always hear to guard your hearts above all else but here we will make it practical. These pillars are essential because the enemy often attacks us in four key areas of our lives: God's love for us, our identities, our freedom/authority, and the eternal promises that God has given us. We can see a vivid example of this in the temptation of Jesus in the desert, as described in Matthew 4. Just before Jesus was baptized and risen, the voice of God declared, "This is my son, the beloved." In the very next chapter, it is important to note that the enemy disregards this declaration and questions Jesus, saying, "If you are the son of God…" Here we can notice how the enemy not only fails to acknowledge Jesus as the beloved but also tries to undermine his identity. Furthermore, the tempter challenges Jesus to turn a rock into bread, attempting to challenge his authority. Lastly, the enemy asks Jesus to bow down to him and he'll have the kingdoms of this world. Jesus responds, "It is written, you shall worship the Lord and serve him only." Here he challenges his freedom. These scriptural pillars serve as a powerful defense against the enemy's attacks. These are the tactics that he used with Jesus and if used against Jesus he is going to use them against us. He used his big guns against the son of man, victory came through firing back with scriptures to defeat him, so it is with us. By understanding and embracing God's love for us, our true identity in Christ, the freedom and authority we have been given through His sacrifice, and the eternal promises He has made, we can stand firm against the temptations and deceptions of the enemy and his fiery darts in our minds. The mind is our true battlefield; we must be armed and ready. So, let us delve into these twelve scriptural pillars, which are foundational to have as we learn how to guard our hearts and live in the fullness of God's love, our true identities, freedom, and eternal promises.

Love	We must know the love of the Father
Identity	We must know who we are in the love of the Father
Freedom	We must know the freedom and authority we possess in our identity in the love of the Father
Eternal Promises	We must know the eternal promises of the Father that are unshakeable

Let's take these LIFE principles and start downloading them into our lives. This is meant to be recited during the morning routine of disruption. It should be used after your time of gratitude. I also encourage you to recite and memorize these verses at night to end your nighttime routine since this is stated in scripture as an instruction. Do not overcomplicate this process. We recommend starting with one verse and adding one additional verse as you see fit. When starting for the first time, add a new verse every 21 days until all 12 verses are memorized. These verses will be recited for the longevity that the Harpu practical practice is followed.

Love

We start with meditating on verses about love. The enemy's biggest weapon in his arsenal is the area of love. He accomplished his will if he could disperse hate from childhood to adulthood. What surfaces as a result of being unloved are the characteristics of offenses: loneliness, bitterness, isolation, anger, and depression, to name a few. Dr. Caroline Leaf continually states that we are wired for love. Behaviors, other than that, are learned behaviors that we have to unlearn. We can unlearn these things by allowing God's truth to penetrate our hearts. There are eight different types of love known to us:

1. Eros - romantic love
2. Philia - affectionate love
3. Philautia - self-love

4. Storge - familiar love
5. pragma - enduring love
6. Ludus - playful love
7. Mania - obsessive love
8. Agape - unconditional love.

God's love, agape, is the only unconditional one mentioned above. The reason we need to have this implanted in our hearts is because we need to remember that he loves us abundantly despite our weaknesses, despite being sinners, and despite being enemies. "For while we were still weak, at the right time Christ died for the ungodly ... but God shows his love for us in that while we were still sinners, Christ died for us ... For if while we were enemies we were reconciled to God by the death of his Son, much more, now that we are reconciled, shall we be saved by his life" (Romans 5:6, 8, 10 ESV).

We must begin to view the world through the lens of God's perfect love. God loves us; from this position, we can love others. Jesus teaches in John 13:34 (VOICE), "So I give you a new command: Love each other deeply and fully. Remember how I have loved you and demonstrate your love for others in those same ways." The unconditional, unhindered love of the Father allows us to be conduits of this love to others.

We love God only as much as the person we love the least. I don't know about you, but this shakes me to the core. This confronts my heart and challenges my definitions of love. We can often love the sinner if their sin wasn't committed against us. I can love the liar if they don't lie to me. I can love the person who gossips if they do not gossip about me. I can love the thief so long as they do not steal from me. Often, we love with conditions, but this is not the love God has deposited in our hearts.

Many of us have been conditioned to love with conditions: "I love you if you prove your love by doing this or that." "I love you, but you must continue this or that." "I love you if you can prove this or that." But God loved us even before we knew him because his love was not based on what we could do but on what he had already done for us. If we can view our shortcomings and hurts from God's agape love (grace), we can get further than ever before. If we can let go of our past hurts by applying this love to others, imagine what can happen after ninety days of practicing the LIFE principle you are learning in this chapter.

When we are limited in our love, it causes us to be limited in the amount of grace we extend to people because we are focused on the shortcomings of others and, therefore, disqualify them with our conditioned love. Think of all the people you have said "I love you" to throughout your life. Are they all still part of your life now? If you consider why some of them aren't around anymore, it's probably because they did something that made you feel they weren't worthy of your love anymore. Your love was conditional, understandably so, since we are humans.

Life is not always fair. Life does not always make things even, and when we feel as though we were cheated, the ego is born to protect our hearts by cutting away those who hurt us. However, when we do this, we demonstrate that we need God's love. If we can love others as God loves us, we can hopefully impart that same love to others.

The art of becoming inner engineers involves knowing that we have to shift certain things in our hearts to see the world according to God's perspective and not humankind's. The only way to effectively do this is to continue to deposit God's love into our hearts. Love must be the lens in which we see the world. We cannot withdraw $1,000 from an ATM if no one has ever deposited the $1,000. We cannot give away something we don't possess. God gives us his agape love in abundance so that we can disperse it in those areas of our lives lacking this love. This will occur as we meditate on God's love: after twenty-one days, we will have created a new way of thinking and new neural pathways. After ninety days, it will be who you become from the heart, let the transformation begin from the inside. As you become one with this truth you will love others the way God loves you.

I made the following spiritual principles personal. Listed below are the three scriptures to meditate on every morning and night as a life habit. Allow yourself to memorize them over time and write these words in your heart.

Scriptural pillars of love:

This is real love—not that I loved God, but that he loved me and sent his Son as a sacrifice to take away my sins. (1 John 4:10 NLT)

Christ proved God's passionate love for me by dying in my place while I was still lost and ungodly! (Romans 5:8 TPT)

So now I live with the confidence that nothing in the universe has the power to separate us from God's love. (Romans 8:38 TPT)

Identity

We are powerful beyond measure. It is our light, not our darkness, that most frightens us. We ask ourselves, who am I to be brilliant, gorgeous, talented, fabulous? Actually, who are you not to be? You are a child of God. You're playing small does not serve the world. There is nothing enlightened about shrinking so others won't feel insecure around you. We are all meant to shine, as children do. We were born to manifest the glory of God that is within us. It's not just in some of us; it's in everyone who believes. And as we let our light shine, we unconsciously permit others to do the same.

Google defines "identity" as "the fact of being who or what a person or thing is." If our identities are wrong, everything we produce will also be wrong. Our identities are what help us define our worth and worthiness. Our identities empower us to move forward or cause us to stay stuck. We must remind ourselves of our identities. I aim to give you the tools to remind you who you are. Meditating on that will create a firm foundation in your heart.

God's first statement concerning us is essential because it sets up God's big picture for our lives. "God spoke: 'Let us make human beings in our image, make them reflect our nature so they can be responsible for the fish in the sea, the birds in the air, the cattle and, yes, Earth itself, and every animal that moves on the face of the earth'" (Genesis 1:26 MSG). God states here that we are created in his image. I remember watching a movie with my daughter called "Ice Age": The Meltdown, which features one of my favorite comedy actors, Ray Romano, as Manny, and Queen Latifah as Eli. In this movie, Manny is a supposedly extinct mammoth until he meets Ellie, the last female Mammoth. The only problem is that since birth, Ellie had been raised with possums and had inherited all the characteristics of possums. She even hangs in a tree like a possum and has the same fears as a possum. When she sees an eagle, she plays dead because she was raised with possums. Even though externally, she was a mammoth that, at the time, dominated the earth because of its size, her mind was conformed to a possum. In one scene, Manny confronts her about her characteristics and her image, and it is not until she sees herself in a mirror that she realizes she isn't a possum but a mammoth. She then accepts her identity and starts moving into the dimension of who she is rather than what she thought she was. Identification is important. We must think equally about who we were created to be.

This is the first statement ever made concerning humankind's identity and purpose. Our identity is Godlike. Psalm 82:6 (AMP) states, "You are gods; Indeed, all of you are sons of the Most High." However, the world will warp this truth, and we often fall victim to it because we all want to be liked. Unfortunately, some of us feel we can be likable only if we please other people, so we change ourselves to do so. This means that authenticity and being true to yourself are sacrificed to be the person you think others want you to be. Living true to yourself and following your values will give you enduring happiness and fulfillment. Just doing what others expect of you is a pathway to boredom.

We live in a culture that prioritizes doing and achieving. This outward focus leaves little time for introspection, insight, and self-knowledge. Dr. Caroline Leaf states, "Scientists are proving that the relationship between what you think and how you understand yourself—your beliefs, dreams, hopes, and thoughts—has a huge impact on how your brain works." (Dr. Caroline Leaf, Switch on Your Brain.)

As you have learned throughout this book, how the brain works is paramount to how our lives are formed. This is why we must ensure that our identities are the correct ones. Finding our identities is foundational to our faith journeys. When we lack the love mentioned above, we lack building our identities internally out of love. Because of this, we seek out our identities in the external media of relationships, success, and acceptance. We then seek validation from our external environment and culture. What people say and think become opinions we live by. We need to avoid seeking externally what can be defined only internally.

Reciting verses will realign our perspectives to see ourselves as kings and queens from the heart. You are not lost. You are not weak. You are not a loser. You are not hopeless. There is a crown that Jesus has set aside just for you. Your identity is one of royalty and power, prestige and favor. Allow God to redefine what the world has misdefined because it didn't know your original definition. You are the image of God.

In the early stages of our lives, our identity begins to take shape. It is during this time that we draw from every experience, starting from the moment we were in the womb, up until adulthood. It is important to reflect on the states of our learning from birth to the age of 28, as they play a crucial role in shaping who we become.

These stages of learning form the foundation of our internal memories, which combine with external experiences to determine our true selves. However, it is crucial to note that without God being at the center of this journey, we become vulnerable to the influence of society. Jesus himself warned us about building our lives on sinking sand, emphasizing the importance of hearing his teachings and applying them to our lives.

In the analogy, Jesus compares those who disregard his teachings to a foolish man who built his house on the unstable sand. When the rain poured, the floods came, and the winds and waves beat against the house, it collapsed and was swept away. Similarly, if we do not anchor our lives on God's truth we become susceptible to the forces of the world, and our identity may crumble under its pressures.

Therefore, it is essential for us to recognize the significance of our early years, the experiences we encounter, and the impact they have on our identity formation. By embracing God's truth and making his word the cornerstone of our lives, we can build a solid foundation that will withstand the storms.

"But everyone who hears my teaching and does not apply it to his life can be compared to a foolish man who built his house on sand. When it rained and rained and the flood came, with wind and waves beating upon his house, it collapsed and was swept away" (Matthew 7:26–27 TPT). This analogy speaks volumes about the importance of building our lives on the solid foundation of God's truth.

As I reflect on my own journey, I realize that it is never too late to start building a solid foundation. God's love and wisdom are always available to us, no matter where we are in life. We can choose to let go of the shifting sands of worldly expectations and instead, anchor ourselves in the truth of God's word. One of the most beautiful aspects of God's teachings is their practicality. They are not meant to be lofty ideals that are impossible to attain. Rather, they are meant to guide us in our everyday lives, helping us navigate through the complexities and challenges that we face. For instance, when we are tempted to judge others harshly, God's teachings remind us to show compassion and understanding. When we are faced with difficult decisions, His word provides us with principles to guide our choices. When we are feeling lost or overwhelmed, His promises offer us comfort and hope.

It is through the internalization and application of these truths that we truly experience transformation. It is not enough to simply know about God's teachings; we must allow them to take root in our hearts and shape our character. In doing so, we find that our lives become more aligned with God's purpose for us. We no longer chase after the empty promises of the world, but instead, seek to live in a way that brings glory to Him. We begin to prioritize love, grace, and forgiveness, recognizing that these are the qualities that truly matter. So, my friend, I encourage you to take a step back from the chaos of the world and take time to build your foundation on the rock of God's truth. Seek His guidance, study His word, and allow His teachings to transform your life. In doing so, you will find peace, joy, and a sense of purpose that surpasses anything the world can offer.

Listed below are the three focus scriptures to meditate on day and night. Allow yourself to memorize them over time, and write these words in your heart.

Scriptural pillars of identity:

God made him who had no sin to be sin for us, so that in him we become the righteousness of God. (2 Corinthians 5:21 NIV)

See what great love the Father has lavished on us, that we should be called children of God! And that is what we are! (1 John 3:1 NIV)

But we are a chosen people, a royal priesthood, a holy nation, God's special possession, that we may declare the praises of him who called us out of darkness into his wonderful light. (1 Peter 2:9 NIV

Freedom and Authority

The word "freedom" is a combination of two words, "free" and "dom," which mean "free dominion." With freedom comes the authority to do what God has called you to do. Since we know when we have freedom in Christ we also have authority because he imparts this to us. Freedom is not just a mere word, but a powerful concept that holds within it the essence of liberation and authority. It is the key that unlocks the door to our true purpose and potential. In this beautiful journey called life, we often find ourselves searching for something more. Something that sets us free from the burdens and limitations that weigh us down. That something is freedom. When we embrace freedom in Christ, we understand that it is not just about being released from bondage, but about stepping into our divine calling. It is about recognizing that we have been granted the authority to fulfill the unique purpose that God has placed within each of us.

God, in His infinite wisdom, created us to reign and dominate freely. He designed us to be co-creators with Him, building a kingdom within us where He is at the center. It is a return to the Garden of Eden, where we can walk in harmony with our Creator, fulfilling our purpose with joy and fulfillment. To fully grasp the magnitude of this freedom, we must meditate on the spiritual principles that guide us. By immersing ourselves in God's word, we not only gain understanding but also become what He intended us to be. His word becomes a solid anchor in every area of our lives, ensuring that our perception is one of victory, regardless of the circumstances we face. So, my friends, let us embrace this gift of freedom. Let us walk confidently in the authority and purpose that God has bestowed upon us. May we be reminded that we are co-creators in this grand tapestry of life, and with God by our side, there is no limit to what we can achieve.

In the realm of freedom, there exists a profound sense of authority. It is through the liberation granted by the Son that we truly become free. This understanding leads us to embrace our Sonship, a vital aspect of our existence. It is crucial to recognize our importance as sons of God, for just as He is, so are we in this world. As children of the Almighty, we have been unshackled and bestowed with power and authority. With this newfound freedom, we are entrusted with the responsibility to liberate others. It is a beautiful cycle - free people, free people.

Understanding the concept of Sonship is paramount. We are no longer slaves but rather sons and daughters of the living God. And with this divine status, He bestows upon us authority. This authority is indispensable; without it, we would be incomplete. God has liberated us from something for something, that being purpose. It is imperative to internalize this principle of freedom and authority. Mere intellectual knowledge is insufficient; it must be engraved within our hearts. If we merely desire something in our minds without it reverberating deeply within our hearts, the deeply ingrained programs from our formative years will prevail. Thus, it is imperative to implant this revelation within the depths of our hearts.

So, let us embrace this understanding of freedom and authority. Let us revel in the knowledge that we are sons and daughters of the Most High. And with this knowledge, let us exercise our authority to free others from the chains that bind them. For with freedom comes authority, and with authority, we can truly make a difference in this world.

Jesus teaches us that we are capable of doing even greater things in his name because he has gone to the Father. Through Jesus, we are freed from the chains of slavery and called to fulfill the purpose that the Father has for us. It is important to understand and firmly establish in our hearts that we can do nothing apart from God. When we receive Jesus, we also receive the Father, enabling us to carry out the tasks that He has assigned to us. This realization brings us true freedom, and it is crucial for us to firmly grasp this concept in our hearts. If we waver in our understanding and still identify ourselves as slaves rather than sons and daughters of God, our minds may lead us back into slavery and uncertainty in our journey. So let us embrace our freedom with a relaxed and peaceful mindset, knowing that in Him, we have the authority to fulfill our purpose.

The main objective of this book has been becoming an inner engineer of our hearts through our God-given abilities. Setting our hearts back to their original settings of love, identity, freedom, and eternal promises we will inevitably begin to bear good fruit in our lives. It is from this place that you will establish your future. The great thing about today is that my past does not have to dictate my future. I can declare that "God uses all things for the good of those who love him and who have been called according to his purpose" (Romans 8:28 NLT).

Imagine being free from your past, free from fear, free to become all God has called you to be, free from darkness, free from judgment, free from bondage. Your perspective and your views of your future will be radically changed by these verses. You have created a foundation that is unshakable. It is from this unshakeable foundation that you will build your new identity in freedom.

Understanding your true identity and that you were created to love are truths that provoke freedom. We are heading into a future based on God's opinion of us, not man's opinion. Jesus speaks about these spiritual principles in John 8:32 (NIV) by saying, "Then you will know the truth, and the truth will set you free."

As stated before, the word "know," in the original Greek, is "kinosko." This word means "To become one with." Meditating day and night is transforming the natural realm and redirecting our lives back to our original settings, which are spiritual. Neuroscience calls this the art of learning. It is termed the quantum Zeno effect, or QZE. This understanding of science is significant because it gives us the ability to be intentional in our process of inner engineering.

I remember going to the eye doctor because I couldn't see clearly, and the doctor sat me down in a chair and put some lenses over my eyes. The doctor kept shifting them, and every shift produced more clarity. What you will be doing by meditating on these spiritual principles is shifting your perspective and your views on life. You have been changing day after day, and everything is becoming clear. I remember my journey, and as I was meditating day and night, I saw a significant change that changed my life and the lives of those around me. I now experience freedom because I have chosen to go back to my original settings and finish what God started from the beginning. This is a very joyful time in my life. I am so happy to have the opportunity to put this in writing and help millions of people get back to their original settings.

Let me end this section by telling you God will make all things new again. He takes the lowly to shame the wise. (See 1 Corinthians 1:27 ESV.) It is not about status, plaques, or titles. It is about the simplicity of being humble before him and allowing him to redirect our lives. Like a GPS, we will never get to another destination unless we change the address. Our hearts are the GPS of the soul, and all you're doing is inputting a new address to get to a new destination.

Listed below are the three focus scriptures to meditate on day and night. Allow yourself to memorize them over time, and write these words in your heart because they possess the freedom and authority God has called us to do.

Scriptural pillars of freedom:

In our union with Christ Jesus he raised us up with him to rule with him in the heavenly world. (Ephesians 2:6 GNT)

As He is, so are we in this world. (1 John 4:17 TPT)

I have given you authority to trample on snakes and scorpions and to overcome all the power of the enemy; nothing will harm you. (Luke 10:19 NIV)

Eternal Promises

The word "eternal" means "Lasting or existing forever; without end or beginning." When Jesus was praying he stated what eternal life was, "Now this is eternal life: that they know you, the only true God, and Jesus Christ, whom you have sent." (John 17:3 NIV) Eternal, abundant, prosperous, peace-filled life begins the day we choose to believe in Jesus. Our original settings begin the day we choose to put our faith in Jesus.

When we speak eternally, it is something everlasting. On this journey, if you establish your heart and mind with the first three life principles, this principle is for the promises to be flowing in your life. God established promises for us so that we may see them and have hope through them.

What are the promises of God? They include peace, joy, sound mind, power, health, and wealth. Have you been lacking in these areas? Well, perhaps many times we don't see God's promises as evident because our foundations are not set on his truth. Our hearts are wavering all over the place based on external signals and emotions that move our cores because of the lack of foundation. Then we start to doubt if GOD is with us, We must be grounded in God's truth and his promises.

It is similar to a tree. We know a tree must be grounded so the roots can support the tree as it grows and, after some time, give forth fruits. Similar to a tree, we ought to be grounded on his truth to allow the roots to penetrate so that in due time the tree bears fruit. What are the fruits? The promises of God in our lives!

We believe that God is with us when we are good and then leaves us when we are bad. This doubt is the killer of relationships with the Father. Anytime we are bad, we think the Father leaves us. That is far from the truth because he is with us until the day we see him by faith. Doubt has been robbing people for centuries. If the enemy can get you to doubt, he's won and the certainty of God's promises in your life is gone because of this wavering belief system.

"But he must ask [for wisdom] in faith, without doubting [God's willingness to help], for the one who doubts is like a billowing surge of the sea that is blown about and tossed by the wind." (James 1:6 AMP). Here the apostle James says that faith without assurance is void. We are asking and not receiving because of doubt! When we doubt, our minds are not in alignment with our hearts. That's why it is so essential to have the scripture in our hearts. When we have assurance and undoubtedly align our hearts with what God says rather than be influenced by emotions, when the mind and the heart are in unison, that's when the Word of God will be dominant in your life. Our hearts have to be anchored on God's words and promises without wavering because of external circumstances.

The battle is within your mind. The conscience will always come against us to separate us from God. Knowing the good and bad keeps us in the judgment of self, and we do this very well. Unless you have the truth that God is for you, then judgment will continue to reign in your life. However, if you download these twelve scriptures, they will be like scud missiles to combat your emotions. When the enemy sends flaming arrows to destroy you, the Word will shoot out of your heart and destroy the arrows in the air before they reach you. No one will get hurt, remember the battlefield is in the mind.

In my studies of ancient traditional Jewish culture, I noticed something very important. A man cannot marry a woman unless he builds her house. Normally the father teaches his son how to build the house. There are three steps in building a house. First one has to start with a foundation. A solid foundation consists of digging a hole and pouring concrete into it. Once it has become solid, then one builds the walls. Lastly, the roof is built and the windows are put into the house. So often we never get to see God's eternal promises of peace, prosperity, health, and wealth. Why? Because we don't lay the proper foundation. The reason for this is that we were never taught how to do it! A strong foundation pertaining to our lives is created when we fix our eyes on Jesus and internalize his truths in our hearts.

Another reason we don't see promises is because of our lack of understanding that God is with us! He is not just for us but in us. That profound truth in our hearts has to be established. We were given the roof, the windows, and the adornments, but we were never shown how to establish the foundation so that we could build the house. The next three verses are key to our growth. Eternal promises are those that are forever. They never change, never switch, and are always available. Eternal promises are the glue that keeps us together. Ever used Krazy Glue? It holds things together that are normally difficult to join. These next three verses are the glue that holds everything together. The fact that if he's with us, no one can stand against us is a powerful eternal truth that resides in us until the day we see him.

Listed below are focus scriptures to meditate on day and night. Allow yourself to memorize them over time, and write these words in your heart.

Scriptural pillars of eternal promises:

Never will I leave you; never will I forsake you. (Hebrews 13:5 NIV)

If God is for us, who can be against? (Romans 8:31 NIV)

So do not fear, for I am with you; do not be dismayed, for I am your God. I will strengthen you and help you; I will uphold you with my righteous right hand. (Isaiah 41:10 NIV)

In the depths of our hearts lies a battlefield, where emotions and truth clash in a never-ending struggle. It is a place where our minds become overwhelmed by the tidal wave of feelings, and reason is drowned in the chaos. But there is a way to change the game, to shift the balance of power in our favor. It begins with the act of downloading scriptures into the very core of our being. These sacred words, imbued with divine wisdom, have the power to transform our hearts and minds. As we internalize them, they become more than just mere words on a page; they become a shield, a sword, and a fortress against the onslaught of emotions. This is not about mere intellectual understanding, for knowledge alone cannot withstand the tempest of emotions. No, it's about something deeper, something more profound. It's about allowing these scriptures to penetrate our hearts, to become an integral part of our very being. It's about cultivating a heart of knowledge that surpasses mere head knowledge. When our hearts are fully engaged in this battle, something incredible happens. The truth, once overshadowed by our emotions, now rises to the surface with an unstoppable force. It becomes the driving force behind our thoughts, our actions, and our decisions. It empowers us to stand firm in the face of adversity, to overcome obstacles, and to walk in the fullness of God's power.

So, my friend, I pray that these principles I've shared with you today will serve as the final piece of your scriptural foundation. May they anchor you in a faith that is unshakable and immovable. May they lead you to encounter the eternal promises of God in your life, and may you walk in the victorious power that comes from a heart fully surrendered to truth. Take a deep breath, my friend, and let these words sink deep into your being. Allow them to transform your heart, renew your mind, and guide your steps back into your original settings. In this battle of the mind, let truth be your compass, and let the power of God within you be your strength.

Printed in the United States
by Baker & Taylor Publisher Services